STUDIES IN MODERN EUROPEAN LITERATURE
AND THOUGHT

General Editor:
ERICH HELLER
Professor of German
in the University College of Swansea

ANTON CHEKHOV

Also published in this Series

Other titles are in preparation

ANTON CHEKHOV

BY

W. H. BRUFORD

NEW HAVEN

YALE UNIVERSITY PRESS

1957

CONTENTS

INTRODUCTION

Fifty years after Anton Chekhov's death at the early age of 44, his reputation seems as firmly established as that of any European writer of the later nineteenth century. In Russia, where he had accomplished the unusual feat of attracting first an unliterary and then a literary public, his stories, to judge by the number and size of editions, are as widely read, his plays as often performed as ever, and numerous critical and biographical studies treat him as perhaps the last of the Russian classic writers. Abroad he has long been regarded as one of the supreme masters of the short story and one of the most original and influential of modern dramatists. In English speaking countries, though the novelty has worn off which made so many of us await with eager expectation each successive volume of Mrs Garnett's translation, his plays are still a challenge to every ambitious producer, the literature about him increases every year and the extent of the living interest in his art as a story-teller is reflected not only in the number of reprints and selections which are called for, but in the unmistakable imitations of his manner which are to be met with on every side.

A reputation which defies so successfully the eroding effect of changing fashions and political tension, both at home and abroad, must rest on a firm foundation, the power to create characters and situations which speak to the imagination of all alike, and this power no one who has written of Chekhov has ever denied. But besides this fundamental appeal of life to life, there are minor sources of interest in Chekhov's work which have been very variously appreciated by his many critics in the different countries in which he has continued to move readers and audiences, notwithstanding changes in critical taste. In Chekhov's own lifetime, the ordinary Russian reader appreciated him first as a humorist, and then as a writer whose pictures of contemporary life were incomparably vivid and completely true in tone. Many, no doubt, like Lenin himself, relished particularly the criticism implied in his satirical sketches of officialdom, though the literary critics often reproached him with painting trifles, with having no heroes, offering no social solutions and spreading despondency. When he became known in England and America, it was the poet of futility that was seen in him, a sensitive, sceptical onlooker, full of pity and longing, who excelled in conveying fleeting moods in plays and stories almost devoid of plot. He was read, as Mr Edmund Wilson has said, 'almost exclusively by a specialized literary public, with

7

whom he has sometimes been a cult and by whom he has been regarded as the master of so exquisite an art, so far from obvious in its themes and technique, that one can only compare the attitude toward him to the attitude toward Henry James at the time when James had not yet come to figure as a pillar of the national pantheon.' In present-day Russia, however, critics present him as a man of the people, a democratic poet whose social conscience made him increasingly ill at ease in pre-revolutionary Russia and who, though himself no revolutionary, devoted himself, according to his lights, to the good of the people, as a herald before the dawn. He is still indisputably a living force, whether as quoted in public, as he was by Stalin not long ago at a party congress, for his castigation of the mean bourgeois vices which, it was said, still persist from Russia's past, or as read at home, for his human and aesthetic appeal and occasionally, one may hope, as the voice of freedom, indignant at any kind of coercion or bureaucratic pedantry.

It is not easy to draw a picture of Chekhov from our own perspective which will reconcile all these different conceptions, each a facet of the truth, but each due in part to the habits of thought which every reader owes to his individual history and social circumstances, and it will be impossible to make the attempt without giving some attention to the development of Chekhov's art and thought, viewed in relation to the Russia of his time.

I

The Potemkin of Literature (1860–1888)

When Chekhov, in 1888, was awarded by the Academy of Sciences a half share of the Pushkin Prize for literature, he described himself to a friend, using a phrase suggested to him by Shcheglov, as an unclaimed child of Fate, a sort of Potemkin, emerging from the wasteland of literature, a bourgeois among the nobility, doomed to an early fall. Early in the previous year, surprised to find long articles about himself in the newspapers, he had written to another friend that he was the only writer up to that time who had gained the attention of the critics through newspaper contributions alone. The public for which he had first written had indeed been the barely literate readers of the illustrated comic weeklies of Moscow and St. Petersburg, and a little later the audiences of unpretentious theatres who delighted in plain farce. Jealous colleagues did not allow his origins to be forgotten during his lifetime and now, of course, Russian children learn at school that his father, an unsuccessful provincial shopkeeper, had been born a serf and that Anton, from his student days on, was the chief support of the family, which had by then moved, to save his father from the debtors' prison, from the decaying port of Taganrog in the south, where Anton had been born, to a Moscow slum. Even during his last three years at the Taganrog Gymnasium his parents, after their departure for Moscow, had been able to do little for him and he had maintained himself by tutoring.

Though he wrote regularly from his first term at the University of Moscow in the autumn of 1879, Chekhov entered the realm of literature properly so called only by gradual stages. He had long given evidence of his imaginative gifts. Even as a boy he had a reputation in his family as a mimic, and his first writing can best be described as a kind of mimicry in words. From his later years at school he had been particularly interested in the theatre. He had tried his hand at short farces and even sketched out a long play called *The Fatherless*, which was apparently worked up at Moscow into *That Worthless Fellow Platonov*, his earliest surviving play, published posthumously. But in writing for the Moscow comic journals he was only following the example of his eldest brother Alexander, who was working his way through college by journalism of this kind. Anton's aim too was to maintain himself as a medical student and to give any help he could to his family, who badly needed it. When

9

he found, to his surprise, that he could produce very easily the kind of thing that editors would accept, he exploited his gift to the utmost, with nothing other than an immediate and lucrative effect in view. But at the same time he was intensely interested in his studies and fully intended to make medicine his career. When his thoughts turned to serious writing which would make him a name, it was a medical dissertation (on the history of medicine in Russia) which he contemplated, with a view to an academic career. It is not surprising that *A Dreary Story* reveals such an intimate knowledge and profound understanding of the academic world, or that Chekhov later attached so much importance to his study of *Sakhalin Island*, a work of careful scholarship which no doubt, in his mind, took the place of the thesis he had never completed.

We can well understand Chekhov's initial disinclination to make a career of literature when we read of the type of writer he met in the offices of the Moscow humorous journals. Apart from chance encounters, as with Leskov in 1883, Chekhov did not know any self-respecting authors until he visited St. Petersburg in 1885, and he had the warning examples of his older brothers Alexander and Nicolai constantly before his eyes. Both had something of the artistic strain evident in their father, whose passion for church music had been such a trial to his sons in their boyhood, when from pure enthusiasm he had made them sing on Saturdays and Sundays, first in the choir which he trained for their local church, and then in private devotions at home. When finally freed from his authority, both boys reacted against his excessive strictness, and though Nicolai had real talent as a painter and Alexander some facility in writing, neither had enough strength of character to discipline himself against the relaxing atmosphere of Moscow bohemianism. Fortunately Anton, besides having greater gifts, had, with all his lightheartedness and love of company, a strong sense of responsibility both to his family and to himself.

Chekhov's beginnings as a writer were far from auspicious. For years he was compelled to do hack work for papers which avoided serious themes like the plague, partly in response to the low tastes of their readers and partly from fear of the strict political censorship exercised in the 'eighties, the disillusioned age which followed the temporary triumph of more liberal views in the period of the great reforms. The number of permissible subjects was very small. One was literary parody, and nearly half of Chekhov's first attempts were in this field—parodies of Victor Hugo and other contemporary writers, Russian and foreign. For the rest, contributors had to keep to the stock subjects from private life, the eccentricities of mothers-in-law, old maids and coquettes, the comic aspects of life in the various seasons of the year, with the recurrent fasts and feasts of the church and the normal routine of social life, schoolgoing and courtship, weddings and funerals, visits to the theatre and friends, and summer holidays in the country. Chekhov's early efforts are distinguished from those of his colleagues, we are told, not so much by any literary talent they reveal as by their avoidance of the only too common scurrilities about actors and other public characters openly mentioned by name. They were excluded by Chekhov from the collected edition of his works and only reprinted after his death. Hardly any of them have been translated. He never spent more than a day on any of his contributions, he said in 1883, and even the editor of the Moscow *Dragonfly*, the first paper to accept his work, told him after a year, in the 'Letter-box' column in which comments were sometimes made on contributions received, that he was withering away without flowering, for lack of self-criticism. What was important to the young student was the fee, five kopecks a line, though he often had much difficulty in collecting it from the less reputable journals. This unduly severe rebuke however led him to return for six months to his first love, the drama, in the hope of getting his play *Platonov* performed at the Little Theatre in Moscow, but again his hopes were disappointed.

From the end of 1882 to 1887 the bulk of Chekhov's work was done for a St. Petersburg humorous weekly of rather higher standing than the local Moscow papers. It was edited by Leykin, an author whom Chekhov had himself read with pleasure as a boy. Leykin had a better eye for Chekhov's talent than his earlier employers and paid him better, but he too would have nothing but very short, humorous and topical contributions, 'country cottage' stories in the summer, for instance, and theatre stories in the winter. As 'Antosha Chekhonte's' contributions soon proved to be a great attraction, Chekhov was allowed to make them slightly longer, up to 150 lines instead of the usual 80, but a story was generally rejected if he let a note of sadness creep in. The great mass of stories and miscellaneous pieces written under such conditions for Leykin and others, some 600 in all by 1887, is naturally of uneven quality, but it includes some which make a deep and lasting impression. These have the quality of a good caricature, the comic heightening, with the utmost economy of means, of something closely observed, so that it makes what Chekhov calls 'an effective protest', a telling criticism of life. A gem like *Sergeant Prishibeyev*[1], for instance, though first cut by Leykin and then rejected by the censor, found its way into another journal and became proverbial, so well did it express the resentment felt by all Russians against the strict coercion exercised upon them. The retired sergeant ferrets out offences where even the police see none, his view being that every kind of action is prohibited which the law does not expressly allow. He cannot see a small group of people talking in a village street without trying to disperse them.

As early as 1883 Chekhov wrote *Fat and Thin*, one of the satirical pictures of officialdom in which he excelled. Subjects of this kind had been common since Gogol's time and had come to be allowed by the censor, if not too outrageous, as a kind of safety-valve. The Chekhov who, as a boy, had convulsed his family by mimicking a village deacon's examination by a bishop, puts before us in three pages, consisting mainly of dialogue, where every tone and gesture conveys a sense of character and its background, two contrasted figures. They are old schoolfriends, who meet unexpectedly after many years and greet each other cordially on a station platform. Both are officials, but when it turns out that the fat man has attained very high rank, the thin man, ten grades below him in the hierarchy, is overcome with awe, together with his meek little wife and gawky son, and quickly exchanges his familiar tone for one of nervous deference which his superior finds disgusting. In dozens of other sketches Chekhov treats similar subjects, always with an ironic undertone so discreet that it is possible for readers to have different views about his attitude towards his characters. This is the Chekhov who laughed heartily at others' jokes (says Bunin) and told his own funny stories without moving a muscle. From the same year 1883 we have *A Daughter of Albion*, in which Gorky sees 'a well-fed squire's mockery of a person lonely and strange to her surroundings', and Derman 'a vivid picture of stupid coarse nationalism', though its main intention is certainly comic. Chekhov cannot at that time have had any contacts to speak of with the nobility—Bunin said after his death that he never really knew these circles well enough to write about them—but that was not necessary for him to give us in an amusing anecdote a variation on the theme of human dignity, presenting it, as Derman says, negatively, by instancing

[1] Titles marked with an asterisk are of stories not included in Mrs Garnett's translation.

one of the innumerable ways in which it was then outraged in Russia. When the squire says of the stiff English governess fishing beside him that she 'doesn't count foreigners as human' he is exactly describing the spirit in which he himself treats her, in stripping stark naked to recover his hook and behaving as if she were not there. In an almost farcical story there is implied not only a strong feeling for humanity, but also that sense of the inescapable separateness of human beings, however close they may be to each other in space, which was to become a central feature in Chekhov's plays. The situation is presented not as a narrative, but mainly in dialogue, as if it were happening before us, as a 'scene', to use Percy Lubbock's term (*The Craft of Fiction*), and the squire's slangy, disrespectful language gains further point by being spoken under the very nose of the person to whom it is applied, the Englishwoman who has not troubled to learn any Russian.

The range of subjects in these early stories is already very wide. Besides parodies and variations on stock themes from other writers there is much that clearly came from Chekhov's own experience, as a schoolboy coaching his juniors at Taganrog (*A Classical Student*, 1883, *The Tutor*, 1884); as a slum dweller in Moscow (*The Old House*, 1887, *A Father*, 1887); as a Moscow journalist (*Hush*, 1886, *Excellent People*, 1886); as a doctor (*Surgery* *, 1884, *A Dead Body*, 1885, *The Examining Magistrate*, 1887, *Enemies*, 1887); as theatre enthusiast (*A Tragic Actor*, 1883, *An Actor's End*, 1886, *The Jeune Premier*, 1886, *Boots*, 1885); as medical expert in court (*In the Court*, 1886, *A Malefactor*, 1885); on his country holidays at Babkino (*The Fish*, 1885, *The Witch*, 1886, *Verochka*, 1887); and on his travels in southern Russia (*Happiness*, 1887, *The Beauties*, 1888, *Uprooted*, 1887). That he had to confine himself to comic subjects had long been irksome to Chekhov before he set about writing his first long serious story, *The Steppe*, in 1887. Even before 1885, when he began to contribute to the *St Petersburg Gazette*, which accepted in the first year *Sorrow*, *The Huntsman* and *Misery*, he had written comparatively few stories which did not make a thoughtful reader see pathos as well as humour in his themes. It was the same in *A Daughter of Albion* or in *Fat and Thin* as in his last 'comedy', *The Cherry Orchard*: the same character and situation might excite now laughter, now a sympathetic sadness.

Sociable and high-spirited as he normally was, especially as a young man, Chekhov was always intensely conscious of the hazards of life. He was more sensitive than most to beauty and order and kindliness, but always aware that the things we value have a weak hold on actual existence. From the beginning his work is full of the pathos of the might-have-been, pictures such as that of the journalist who has become a slave to drink and routine, instead of the distinguished author he had hoped to be (*Horse and Tremulous Doe**, 1885), or the composer degenerated into a dance pianist (*The Dance Pianist**, 1885). Even in a commonplace character like the peasant in *A Malefactor*, who uses bolts from the railway as sinkers for his fishing lines, there is in his wrong-headed and comic explanations of his conduct a touching enthusiasm for fishing as something good in itself; similarly with the *Dreams* (1886) of a vagabond, a victim of life, and with innumerable other characters, including ineffective social idealists like *Ivanov* in Chekhov's first important play. It is this autumnal mood of melancholy over lost opportunities or the fragility of happiness which gives to even his greatest stories and plays their characteristic colouring. When these human failures have no trace of idealism, they are comic and sometimes slightly contemptible, like most of the actors in the early sketches and many of the officials, but then, as we have seen, they may still draw attention to the ideal of human dignity by displaying so clearly its opposite.

Both in his realism and in his humane sympathy Chekhov was of course continuing a Russian literary tradition, under the direct influence of Gogol and Goncharov, Turgeniev and Tolstoy. 'People are not good or bad; they are only more or less unhappy and deserving of sympathy—this may be taken as the formula of all the Russian novelists from Turgeniev to Chekhov' (Mirsky). Chekhov took his subjects from contemporary life—there seems to be only one story set in the past, *A Story Without a Title*, and that has clearly a contemporary application, against Tolstoyanism—and he was conscious of no conflict between his scientific interests as a medical man and his ideals as a writer. The study of medicine had opened his eyes, he felt, to much in life that he would otherwise have missed; it had given him a keener sense of truth. He claimed to be primarily an observer, one who did not 'rush into anything with only his imagination to draw upon.' Like Goethe, he believed that nature had more inventive genius than he had.

But to create living characters who move us as his do, he needed more than the power to observe closely and to 'conquer his squeamishness'. He saw his real life subjects with the eye of a humane and thoughtful student of society and an artist, who could only work well when he stood well back from his subject, as it were, and saw it in proper perspective, so that he could convey 'a feeling of the human mass out of which his figures had come, the atmosphere and background', to use his own approving description of some stories of Gorki's. 'You should only sit down to write,' he told Bunin, 'when you feel as cold as ice.' This is how he expressed in his maturity the same doctrine of 'aesthetic distance' as is implied in a criticism of his brother Alexander's work as early as 1883, in which he warns him against expressing his own personal feelings, instead of evoking characters which exist in their own right.

To achieve mastery as he did, Chekhov needed not only the support of a literary tradition. He had to acquire a sense of personal freedom and to achieve a personal style. His much-quoted letter to Suvorin in 1889, when he felt himself to be at last on the right road, shows how consciously he had tried, by following an ideal, to make up for what he lacked as a man of the people, unsupported by religious faith. To be a good writer, he says,

... in addition to abundance of material and talent, some-thing else, no less important, is necessary. One needs, in the first place, to be mature, and further, to have the feeling of personal freedom, a feeling that has only recently begun to spring up in me. What took its place earlier was my lightheart-edness, carelessness and lack of respect for my work. What writers of gentle birth received from nature for nothing, we others have to earn at the cost of our youth. Write a story of how a young man, the son of a serf, who has served in a shop, sung in a choir, and had a secondary school and university education, who has been brought up to respect rank and office, to kiss priests' hands, to bow to other people's ideas, to say thank you for every piece of bread, who has often been whipped, who has trudged from one pupil to another without galoshes, who has been accustomed to fighting, and tormenting animals, who has been glad to be asked out to dinner by rich relations and played the hypocrite before God and men without any need, simply from awareness of his own insigni-ficance—write how this young man squeezes the slave out of himself drop by drop until, waking one fine morning, he feels himself to have a real man's blood in his veins, and not a slave's.

Exactly when and under what influences Chekhov began to take his writing seriously it is difficult to say. His inward growth

15

-was met, no doubt, by influences from without, especially praise from writers whom he esteemed. When Leskov visited Moscow in 1883, Leykin brought Chekhov into touch with him, and it became clear that things like *A Daughter of Albion* had made a deep impression on that highly original writer, whom Chekhov greatly admired. In a droshke one evening after a party, Leskov, then 53 and at the height of his powers, said to his young companion: 'I anoint you with oil as Samuel anointed David, and say to you, "Write!"' But what impressed Chekhov far more than this initiation, for he knew that Leskov was not too sober at the time, was the encouragement he received from leading literary men in St. Petersburg on his first visit in December 1885, after the publication of *The Fish* and *The Huntsman* in the *Petersburg Gazette* in the summer of that year. Suvorin, editor of the *New Times*, the leading Russian newspaper, began to take his stories and to offer him advice and criticism, and in the following March Chekhov was surprised to receive a letter from the highly respected novelist Grigorovich, who had greatly admired the character-drawing and the descriptions of nature in *The Huntsman*. To be told that he had 'real talent, which placed him far above the rest of his generation' was overwhelming for one hitherto so unambitious. His literary acquaintances would laugh in his face if they heard anything of the kind, Chekhov replied, and his family was always urging him not to sacrifice his profession to scribbling. His medical work still took up much of his time, he said, and he wrote only when free in the daytime, and for part of the night.

The five longer stories published in the *Petersburg Gazette* and the *New Times* up to March 1886 are indeed the work of a real artist. They had been written for the most part during the summer months at Babkino, where the Chekhovs spent their holidays in a cottage on the estate of the Kisselevs, the first aristocratic family Chekhov had really known, charming people with good taste and a large circle of artistic friends, among whom Levitan, the landscape painter, became particularly important for Chekhov. The country round about, in the Moscow province, was already well-known to the Chekhovs from several visits to Voskressensk, a couple of miles away, where Anton's younger brother Ivan had until recently been a schoolmaster and able to put them up in his official quarters. Chekhov had made the acquaintance of the artillery officers stationed there, and so found the background for *The Kiss* (1887) and later for *The Three Sisters*. He had also helped the doctor in charge of the zemstvo hospital near by at Chikino, and taken temporary charge of another hospital in the same district.

All five are stories of country life, although the more sordid aspects of the Russian village are not so prominent as in *Peasants, In the Ravine*, etc., written in the 'nineties, when Chekhov had lived for years in a small village and gained an intimate knowledge of its life through the demands made on his medical skill. There is a holiday atmosphere in some of these earlier country stories, but though some features are idyllic, there is no suggestion of idealisation, and there are already clear hints of the suffering and squalor inseparable from the Russian peasants' lot. The most light-hearted is the first of the series, an elaboration of an incident which actually happened at Babkino when a bathing pavilion was being constructed. As usual, a scene is enacted before us, and half of the humour lies in the comic and completely natural turns of phrase in the dialect of these joiners and estate servants as one after another of them goes down into the water to try to dislodge an eel-like fish from tree-roots under the bank of the river, instead of getting on with his proper work. Finally the master himself joins in, just as eager for a fish as the rest of them—indeed as Chekhov himself, for it is clearly a fisherman's story—but the slippery turbot eludes them all. Here what happens in the story is trifling, and the effect depends on Chekhov's skill in conveying the general atmosphere of a lazy summer's day, the excitement of the participants and the suggestion of contrasted characters through the casual words they speak. Description is reduced to a minimum, but the opening lines bring summer before us, mainly through the sounds of its wild creatures: 'A summer morning. There is not a sound in the still air but the gentle creaking of a grasshopper on the river bank, and somewhere the timid purring of a turtledove. Feathery clouds float motionless in the sky, looking like sprinkled snow.'

In *The Huntsman* the description of the setting is a little fuller, in the anthropomorphic manner common in the early stories, which Chekhov later criticised in Gorki and avoided himself: 'The grass, burnt up by the sun, looks at you sadly, hopelessly. Even if rain should come now, it is too late for it to become green again. The wood stands silent, motionless, as if it were looking intently in a certain direction and expecting something.' The huntsman is described fully too, because his clothes and his way of walking are indications of his character. Except for a few lines at the end, the rest is all conversation, between this handsome young fellow, whose skill makes him an indispensable servant and raises him above his fellow-villagers, and the adoring wife he abandoned long ago for another woman. It would be misleading to describe this as a story without a plot, for this one scene reveals to us the tragedy of a marriage arranged twelve years earlier by a jealous master, out of spite. We see only a late stage in a series of events, but the antecedents are brought out gradually in natural conversation, exactly as in an analytical drama of the French classical type, and we are led to imagine what will certainly follow.

There is a similar time-perspective in the other three tales, and from them all we receive the impression of suffering, tragic in its inevitability, resulting from the clash of two or three perfectly natural characters in circumstances typical of Russian village life. In *Agafya* and *The Witch*, the theme is again the unsatisfied feelings of a woman, in a community where marriages are arranged without regard to sentiment. In *Agafya* the author tells us in the first person about a rendezvous he witnesses, on a warm summer night, between a young woman and a peasant who, like the gamekeeper, has contrived to escape from the common lot of his fellows, in this case by sheer persistence in idleness, so that he has been given the old man's task of scaring birds and cattle from the unfenced village vegetable gardens. A strong, handsome, intelligent fellow, he neither ploughs nor sows, and takes no thought for the morrow, yet some gift of food always comes his way, for he is such a favourite with the village women that he can even treat them with a certain contempt. Again the unusual central character has to be described at length, and the rest is what the narrator, as he is waiting for the fish to rise, sees and hears while he chats with the idle but fresh-minded Savka, after sunset, about the nightingale and the corncrake and the migratory habits of birds. By skilfully selecting evocative detail Chekhov makes us conscious of the passing of time throughout the night, and the personal charm of the care-free Savka works on us too. For the moment, the behaviour of this parasite and an infatuated village girl seems as innocent, or as non-moral, as that of the birds calling in the woods. Then after dawn, we are made to hear her young husband, back from his work on the railway, calling her name on the other side of the river, and to see her crossing the ford, and first hesitantly and then defiantly advancing towards him. No moral judgment is suggested, the future is left to our imagination, yet we feel the story to be complete.

In *The Witch* there is nothing idyllic. Again a revealing scene allows us to imagine the past and the future of an ill-assorted couple, a repulsive old parish clerk and the young wife whom he had taken over, as so often happened then, with her father's post. Whenever a young man asks for shelter on a stormy night, in their single-roomed lodge beside the highway, the husband jealously imagines his wife to have brought the intruder there with the help of the devil. As he feels the devil's hand to be behind the gale that rages outside in the last days of winter, the personification in the initial description in this tale is especially effective, for we seem to see nature through the old man's ignorant and superstitious eyes. Again the length of the night is cleverly suggested, the sounds heard inside as the post coach tries in vain to find the post house, the stages in the brief romance between the young postilion and the wife, and the final altercation between man and wife, opening up the vision of a hopeless future.

The Requiem combines the country setting with another milieu with which Chekhov had been familiar from his boyhood, that of the local church. Though he was by this time an unbeliever, with unpleasant memories of his choir-boy days, he always handled ecclesiastical themes with singular delicacy. The conversation between Father Gregory and the pharisaical old shopkeeper, and the shopkeeper's reflexions during the ensuing requiem for his actress-daughter, are again equivalent to the story of a life. Every detail conjures up a background of manners peculiarly Russian, the lackey almost cut off from his family, his daughter learning with his master's daughters all a lady's accomplishments and taken by them to Moscow, the father's indignation when she returns on holiday and tells him, with his narrow religious views, that she is an actress, and her emotion on seeing again her native countryside, which to him meant nothing at all. The quite short descriptive passages are not stuck on like patches; they reinforce the human interest, adding greatly to the emotional effect of the story, as in its concluding lines: 'And it seems as if together with the incense, the soul of the dead girl is rising in the light. The wisps of smoke, like a child's curls, circle and rise to the window, and it is as if the despondency and grief which had filled that poor soul to overflowing were dispersing too.'

1886, the year in which Chekhov began to contribute to the *New Times*, was the last of three years in each of which he produced well over a hundred stories and articles. Already less than half of his work had appeared in *Fragments*. In another two years the total had dropped to twelve, because he was spending much more time on his stories and increasing their length. The fifty-five stories of 1886 translated by Mrs

Garnett give us a good idea of Chekhov in this period of transition. One is struck in the first place by the extraordinary range of his subjects, though all are taken from contemporary Russian life. This young man of twenty-six can show us, from his Babkino experiences, a feckless but fastidious aristocratic landowner and his neighbour, an heiress without beauty or delicacy of feeling (*A Trivial Incident*), a nobleman with a talent for believing which drives him restlessly from one exaggerated form of idealism to another (*On the Road*), and a household where a hen-pecked husband steals his wife's jewelry and stands by while she searches the governess's room (*An Upheaval*). He can enter with equal sympathy into the mind of a young lay-brother, grieving for the loss of the gentle and gifted monk who had written such inimitable songs of praise (*Easter Eve*). In the monk with his instinctive artistry in words there is clearly much of Chekhov himself, but he can write with convincing sympathy too of the contemplative life, and of the ritual of Easter Eve, the great festival of the Orthodox Church, while we are conscious throughout the story of the tension we have already encountered in Chekhov's work, between the calm, enduring beauty of nature and the insecurity of human life and values. In the same field as this story and *The Requiem* we find *Art*—orthodox ritual again, the blessing of the waters—and *A Nightmare*, where the pathetic poverty of a conscientious young village priest is gradually realised by a self-satisfied official, the narrator, in whose mouth the story runs no risk of becoming sentimental.

Besides the nobility and the church, we have the army, in *The Husband*, where we see the excitement of the ladies of a small town when a cavalry regiment on manoeuvres passes through and its officers dance with them at a ball. As usual, one small typical incident occupies the foreground, but much of the effect results from the atmosphere evoked, which anticipates in some ways that of *The Three Sisters*. Then there is the civil service. Officialdom had been fully exploited by Chekhov in the comic papers in earlier years. In this vein we still have *Ladies*—where a director of education, against his better judgment, gives way to feminine influence in appointing a new clerk—and a much more finished study, *The Privy Councillor*, in which the holiday visit of a high official from St Petersburg to his sister in the country is described by his small nephew. The subject offers many opportunities for comedy in the contrasting of town and country manners, and they are fully used, but even for the boy, of whom so little notice has been taken, there is something pitiful about the uncle's age and loneliness, and when he says goodbye, he jumps into the carriage and hugs the old man affectionately.

A medical student and several kinds of professional men are drawn with the same mingling, in varying proportions, of the gay and sad. *Anyuta* sits patiently in the cold while the young medical student, the fifth one she has lived with, marks in her ribs with charcoal, as he prepares for his anatomy examination. In *Hush!*, *Ivan Matveich* and *Excellent People* we meet a few writers, all self-conscious and vain, expecting deference and every attention from those who live with them. Artists who talk too much and work too little appear in *Talent*, and in three or four theatre stories (*An Actor's End*, *The Chorus Girl*, *The Jeune Premier*) the actors and actresses are drawn as drunken, quarrelsome and lazy. These are all second-rate representatives of the intelligentsia, but Chekhov is not kind, on the whole, to the intelligentsia in general, either here or later. Though he refrains from direct moral judgments, the reader cannot help noticing a lack of human feeling and delicacy in the members of the free professions. The lawyers in *In the Court* exhibit these traits. It is less surprising to find them in the provincial shopkeepers and bank directors of *A Misfortune*, or the wretched pedagogues in a school run by a factory (*The Teacher*), so much like one where Ivan Chekhov had taught for a time.

But the real subject in this last story is the effect on the guests, at the annual dinner given by the factory director to the school staff, of their knowing that the teacher Sysoev is mortally ill, and the reaction of the doomed man himself to the truth that he reads for the first time in their eyes. This was a feeling into which Chekhov could unfortunately enter only too well, at this early stage in his career. He had begun to spit blood in 1884, and shown possible symptoms of consumption even a year earlier. He persuaded others, and apparently himself, that his illness was not serious, and refused to undergo treatment. Perhaps it was unconscious self-deception, or perhaps lack of faith in current remedies. When, after three years of uneasiness, he found himself still alive, he thought, as was commonly believed by medical men then, that if he had stood it for so long, the disease could not be tuberculosis at all, and he wrote confidently to Suvorin about it in 1888. It was only when, in 1897, after repeated warnings, a serious attack in a Moscow restaurant made immediate nursing-home treatment necessary, that he submitted to the orders of his colleagues. Yet he knew all the time how unreliable a guide a patient's own feelings are, for we read in a letter of 1893: 'The enemy that kills the body comes usually imperceptibly, wearing a mask. When you are ill with consumption, for example, it seems to you that it is not consumption, but a mere trifle, and it is the same with cancer. The really terrible is what you are not afraid of!'

It is no narrow section of Russian society to which we are introduced, it is clear, even in the selection of stories of this one year which have been translated, and in his total work there is an even wider sweep, so wide that in the year of his death, a Russian critic could call him 'the most authoritative historian of the last twenty years'. Even before one has read widely enough in him to appreciate this, one is impressed above all by his power of re-creating everyday life as it is lived, not by any particular class, but by everyone. This gift of his is displayed in all the 'trifles from life', pictures from the private lives of ordinary middle-class people, which continue to predominate in his work in 1886. Some are just amusing anecdotes, like *In the Dark*, *A Blunder*, *A Joke*, *The Happy Man*, *A Tripping Tongue*—the titles themselves lead us to expect no more. The husbands and wives, the loving couples, the parents and children of these tales are convincing types, and the interest depends on some little unexpected twist of events, as when a husband, wakened at night by his wife, to find out whether a suspicious figure she has seen through the window is the fireman who visits their cook, gropes his way to the kitchen and finds the cook apparently alone, but when he strikes a match on his return, they see that instead of his own dressing-gown, left with the cook for repair, which he thought he had picked up in the kitchen, he is wearing a fireman's greatcoat. These little tales are masterly in their concentrated realism, their racy, inventive idiom, but they do not open new windows on life, as do the maturer stories and even some of the less hurriedly written products of this year and earlier.

Written at this time for instance, in addition to *The Requiem* and several other stories already discussed, are some stories about children (*Grisha*, *Children*, *Vanka*) composed at the suggestion of Bibilin, the secretary of Leykin's journal, who could appreciate Chekhov's true distinction much better than Leykin himself. The stories about children make up a whole volume in Mrs Garnett's translation (*The Cook's Wedding*). They show us sometimes children amongst themselves, sometimes the world of grown-ups freshly seen from a child's angle, with its conventions laid bare. These stories are notably successful. In spite of the satirical intention in the second group, the children are perfectly natural children, not little philosophers, and it is left to us to draw critical inferences. It was not only the quality of his imagination which enabled Chekhov to write such things, but his unspoilt simplicity, praised by Tolstoy and Gorki. He had 'the innocent eye' and the knack of making even his most affected visitors become their real selves with him and talk of what genuinely interested them. Social criticism is clearly implied for instance in *Vanka*, a picture of child labour under coarse-grained craftsmen, an anticipation of the better-known story *Sleepy*. *A Trifle from Life* refines on this method and shows a broken home from three angles at once, that of the lover, that of the small son of his mistress and that of the unhappy father, separated from his wife and children, but the chief stress is laid on the contrast between the child's keen sense of honour and the thoughtless way in which the lover breaks his promise to the boy 'not to tell'.

It goes without saying that most of Chekhov's pictures of family life turn on the relations of man and woman. He can draw happy souls like *The Darling*, who is devoted to each of a number of husbands in turn and successively adopts the interests of each, but the comedy here is precisely in the multiplicity of her attachments. Usually it suits his purpose better to draw unhappy marriages and random relationships. They furnish better material for the 'vaudeville' type of plot which he often said he was seeking, and which evidently seemed to him to express best the kind of emotion which the spectacle of ordinary life evoked in him, an inextricable tangle of gaiety and sadness. The tension between the two seemed to him the very essence of human experience. What he understood by vaudeville was, however, not everybody's idea of it, and it is illustrated in the following anecdote. 'Someone ought to write a vaudeville like this,' he said one day in the early 'nineties, when a friend had visited him on his farm and they had taken shelter from the rain in an old grain-drying kiln. 'A young couple take shelter in a place like this, laughing and joking, and while they are drying their umbrellas he proposes and is accepted. The rain blows over, the sun comes out, and suddenly he falls dead of heart-failure.' 'But good heavens!' the friend said, 'how can you make a vaudeville out of that?' 'Why, it's like that in life,' Chekhov answered. 'Don't things like that happen? We joke, laugh, and suddenly—flop, the end.'

Here we have again, jokingly expressed, the tragic feeling of the insecurity of all that we hold dear, of which we have found traces in some of the earliest of Chekhov's stories. In 1886 we find things like *A Trifle from Life* or *The Chemist's Wife*, with the same bitter-sweet flavour. They may appear to the reader funny, or cynical, or tragic, according to his idea of life and his present mood. Chekhov rarely indicates his own attitude plainly. He often insisted—for instance, in a letter to a friend about the story *Mire*, another product of 1886 — that it is the artist's business simply to present a picture, not to interpret it, in the sense of taking sides morally. 'A writer,' he said, 'must be as objective as a chemist,' and remember that 'the evil passions are just as much a part of life as the good ones.' *Mire* presents sexual passion as an element in experience just as inexplicable, just as irrational, as death itself. The handsome young lieutenant who calls at a distillery to collect a debt for his brother finds everything in the house ugly and pretentiously squalid. The untidy Jewess who has just inherited the business is cynical and unprepossessing in the extreme, yet even after she has robbed him by a trick of the vital bill of exchange, physical contact with her in the attempt to recover it so intoxicates him that he stays to lunch and returns empty-handed to his brother on the following day. The indignant brother goes to assert his rights and also fails to return. When he does at last arrive, we are shown the pair of them in paroxysms of laughter, and one visit does not satisfy either.

This is the objectivity of a disillusioned, naturalistic age, the kind of thing we find in Maupassant, whom Chekhov admired. As we shall see, there were times later when it did not satisfy Chekhov himself, and when he expressed his admiration for an art, denied, he thought, to himself, 'in which we feel, besides life as it is, the life which ought to be,' an art expressing a definite philosophy of life. It was precisely during the years when he was still consciously educating himself as a serious artist that he was most attracted by Tolstoyan ideas, and sometimes sacrificed imaginative truth to abstractions. But all his search for a philosophy did not alter the main features of the technique he had acquired in the hard school of the humorous journals, and there is no sudden break in the narrative style of Chekhov after 1886, only a growing sureness of touch and maturity of outlook in a smaller output of longer stories, which, however, never become novels.

The first lesson he had had to learn was to be brief, and of this brevity, at first required of him by the editors for whom he worked, he made a virtue. Economy of means is an outstanding characteristic of Chekhov's art. Comparing him with

Turgeniev, for instance, one feels, as Derman says, that the older writer left too little free play to the reader's imagination. This is not an adverse criticism of Turgeniev, who followed quite other aims, but a recognition of a change in our tastes. Through practice, for his first attempts were discursive enough, Chekhov acquired a remarkable feeling for scale in the really short story. Artistic truth, as Hilaire Belloc said, is largely a matter of scale. You can write history, he claimed, or draw a landscape, on various scales with equal truth, representing an object now by a single line, or, when everything else is in proportion, by a whole complex of lines. Chekhov became a master of concise writing, just as some engravers, like Chodowiecki, became masters of book illustration, and like them he had difficulty in drawing on a bigger scale. This is perhaps why, in spite of several attempts, he never succeeded in producing a full-length novel. He never tired of urging other writers to be brief too. In his first conversation with Bunin he advised him, when he had finished a short story, to cut out the beginning and the end. He himself would cut his stories ruthlessly in proof and his plays even in the final rehearsal.

Growing, as they did, out of anecdotes and sketches restricted to a hundred lines or less, Chekhov's stories do not depend for their effect on the invention of a series of happenings. Some make use of surprises, or of merely verbal wit, but there is not the kind of tension in them which makes us ask breathlessly: 'What happened next?' He is concerned, like every story-teller, with people in situations, but he extracts the greatest possible interest out of one or two situations at a time, choosing, as we have seen, a pregnant moment, from which the past is revealed and the future suggested. In showing us people in a particular situation, he tells us what kind of people they are and what kind of world they live in.

Chekhov early became known as a master of 'mood'. He conveys to us the feeling-tone of his figures, their shifting, elusive emotional reactions, not only to one or two distinct objects in their neighbourhood, but to the vaguely seen surroundings, the past and the future. We feel the climate of their soul on a particular morning. It is the kind of thing that Russian and German poets in particular have constantly tried to express, in the first person, in verse. But these characters seem to reveal themselves largely unconsciously, not by deliberate self-analysis, but by what they say or do. In *Vanka*, *A Nightmare* or *Happiness*, for instance, short 'scenes' and narrative passages are followed by longer passages of self-revelation in a letter, or in the omniscient author's reading of their thought, with an effect approaching that of the 'stream of consciousness' technique.

This lyrical effect is often heightened by descriptions of nature, always brief and subordinated to the general theme of the story, not purple patches that hold up the action. What Chekhov aimed at was that every detail mentioned should have a function in the story as a whole. 'If in chapter I you say there was a gun hanging on the wall,' as he put it to Bunin, 'in chapter II or III you must see that it goes off.' In the early stories even the landscapes are often made comic, as well as vivid, by unexpected comparisons, as of a three-windowed cottage with an old woman wearing a night-cap. In 1896 he recommended comparisons with human actions to Alexander as a method of bringing nature to life, but as has been mentioned, he had a distaste for this trick later. 'The sea does not laugh or cry,' he said to Tikhonov in 1902, criticising Gorki, 'it roars, splashes, glistens. See how Tolstoy does it: the sun just rises and sets, the birds sing. There is no laughing and sobbing. Simplicity is what we need.' In the same letter to his brother he had recommended the use of evocative detail, such as 'A piece of glass from a broken bottle shining like a little star on the dam of the water-mill,' to suggest moonlight, but Magarshack thinks that when he makes Trigorin use this same example in *The Seagull*, Chekhov's intention is ironical, as this device seems to him now a little artificial. It is commoner anyhow in his early writings. But throughout he uses landscape emotionally, either to hint at wider horizons contrasted with the foreground happenings, or to underline the prevailing mood. He is particularly fond of the contrast between an all-too-human theme and the serenity of nature, a contrast Graham Sutherland expresses when he paints his thorns, symbols of cruelty, against a blue sky. An example, in Chekhov, anthropomorphic, with effective use of small details, is the beginning of *Mire*: 'The sun smiled gaily on the lieutenant's stars, on the heaps of broken glass scattered about the courtyard. It was all bathed in the bright, healthy beauty of a spring day, and nothing hindered the young green shoots, in which the sap was rising, from trembling and casting shy glances at the bright blue sky.' The 'healthy beauty' out of doors throws into relief the ugly, overpoweringly scented interior of the house and the grossness of the Jewess and her victim. There is a similar contrast later in *A Nervous Breakdown*, between the fresh snow and the brothel scenes, and in *Peasants* between the idyllic scene by the river, near the beginning, and life in the dark, noisy, fly-infested cottages.

26

In the general texture of his writing Chekhov, by 1886, had achieved great simplicity and concentrated expressiveness. 'Brevity is the sister of talent', he told his brother. 'If I write: "A man was sitting on the grass," ' he said to Gorki in 1899, 'it is clear. But it is hard to take in if I write: "A tall, narrow-chested man of medium height with a red beard was sitting down on green grass already trodden down by many passers by, was sitting silently, meekly, looking nervously about him." ' Simplicity is, of course, particularly necessary in dialogue, if it is to sound natural, and the greater part of most of his early stories consisted of dialogue. In the dialogue Chekhov, the accomplished mimic, commonly gives his characters peculiarities of phrasing and pronunciation, as was pointed out in *The Fish*, but this is a less marked feature in his later stories, where the language is so far normalised that Mirsky asserts (with some exaggeration) that all Chekhov's characters speak the same language, his own.

II

The Stories of Chekhov's Maturity

According to Mirsky, *The Party* (1888) is the first story in the typical Chekhovian manner, the biography of a mood, developing under the pinpricks of life, but due in substance to a deep-lying physiological or psychological cause, here Olga's pregnancy. This description, one feels, does not do justice to *The Party*. It is far more than the 'biography of a mood'. It is a convincing picture of a day or two of crisis in Olga's life, in which we get to know her completely as she is to herself, or so we feel, and to almost the same extent to understand her husband and their deepest feelings for each other. This understanding is conveyed to us, not by description and analysis, but by the presentation of a transparent sample of her life, in which her memories and thoughts about the past, her hopes and fears for the future, are as important as the description of her present actions and feelings. It is a chapter in her life so fully realised and so skilfully presented that one is reminded of *Anna Karenina* or *War and Peace*.

Chekhov still has the 'mania for brevity', as he writes to Suvorin in 1889, but he gives more attention than ever to the total shape of the story, the integration of all its parts. The framework is the author's first thought, he said with reference to *The Party*. From the crowd of characters he selects one to be painted in detail, 'scattering the others over the canvas like small change'. But though everything is brought into relation with Olga, we do not see things and people through her consciousness except when it suits Chekhov's purpose, his methods of presentation being very varied. The first of the five sections of a 50-page tale is opened by half a dozen lines of introductory narrative. 'After the birthday dinner, with its eight courses and endless conversation, Olga Michaelovna, whose husband was celebrating his birthday (nameday), went into the garden. Through the strain of smiling and talking continuously, the clattering of the dishes, the clumsiness of the servants, the long pauses between courses, and the discomfort of wearing a corset to hide her pregnancy from the guests, she was completely exhausted.' Chekhov is showing us, as in so many earlier stories, the last stage of a long process, but in this more complex study he does not proceed directly from the introductory narrative to a scene, but throws further light on the central character and the situation by telling us what was passing through Olga's mind, her tender thoughts of 'a little creature of indeterminate sex', interweaving them with deft touches of description of the weather, the shady side-path, the spider that caresses her cheek, and with her unpleasant recollections of the discussions at table. Hearing approaching footsteps, she goes into a garden hut out of the way. The oppressive atmosphere of the afternoon reflects and partly explains her state of mind. The conversation which she overhears between her husband and a girl of seventeen is given as a scene, but we hear it with her mental comments, and in it her husband recalls the incidents leading up to an approaching legal inquiry, which is on his mind the whole time. In this way narrative, scene and the stream of thought all have their function in building up the reader's understanding of a most complex relationship, for man and wife love each other profoundly, but are temporarily at cross purposes, partly because of Olga's condition, partly as a consequence of her husband's childishly self-important behaviour. She is not really cattish nor is he inconsiderate, but before they can find their way back to each other, the tension between them must rise to breaking point and the physical strain on Olga must be relieved. The psychological subtlety with which Chekhov imagines every stage in their quarrel, and its culmination in a fit of hysterics which prematurely brings on Olga's labour, is for some tastes, to use Oliver Elton's phrase, 'over-clinical', but while it produces the impression of that 'absolute and honest truth' which was now Chekhov's primary aim, his treatment of his characters is not the merciless or coldly indifferent analysis of a specimen in a glass case which many more recent authors have practised. There are limits, too, to what is revealed, and we are not shown such things as we could not bear anyone to know about ourselves. Moreover, variety is constantly supplied by the background figures, first by the guests at the interminable party, and then by the many figures which hover about Olga during her confinement, especially the gardener's wife Varvara, with her queer superstitious practices and oddly pronounced words, who in her imperturbability is such a comfort to her over-refined mistress in this commonplace business of child-bearing.

Chekhov's educated characters have the divided soul which is the mark of modernity. Olga is insincere among all her tiresome guests, because convention demands of her a forced gaiety and friendliness, and she works herself up into a fury with her husband, in spite of her love for him, because his own worries have made him more self-absorbed than ever, so that peculiarities which she would normally laugh at get on her nerves, overwrought as she is through her fear and uncertainty and the physical discomfort of her approaching first confinement. But while she is accusing him of hating her because he envies her wealth, a voice within persistently whispers 'feminine logic', and she is as much pained by her own insincerity as by his. Such characters are not so hopelessly at odds with themselves as more recent creations, like those of Kafka and the Existentialists. They remember their former wholeness of mind and can hope to recover it, while the outside world, though it puzzles them by its contradictions, is not yet a heap of disintegrated fragments. Though they have little or no support from religion, there is some semblance of order in society, and they have at least a good nursery behind them.

In the great stories which follow, varying in length between 15 and 150 pages or so, two kinds of interest predominate, singly or combined: the psychological and the sociological. Sometimes, as in *The Party*, our attention is directed to a single character, fully displayed to us from within and without, and always depicted in a particular situation in contemporary Russia. An individual stands out 'like the moon among the stars', as Chekhov said about *The Party*, or as a 'round' character among 'flat' ones, to use Mr E. M. Forster's terms. Sometimes it is a group of people, or a member of a social group, in their typical relation to other groups. The same kind of distinction can be made, as we have seen, among the earliest stories. There are more fully developed examples of each kind from about 1886. *The Kiss* (1887), for instance, represents the first kind, and *A Nightmare* (1886), the second, with its study of a village priest, where we think as we read of the class he belongs to in society just as much as of the individual.

From *The Party* onwards, we have Chekhov's work at its maturest and best in both types, and because he always sees his figures with 'the human mass out of which they came', all belong in some degree to both types. *A Nervous Breakdown* (1888) is primarily a study of a temperament similar to that of the Russian writer Garshin, who had just died by his own hand, and for whose memorial volume the story was written, a man morally sensitive to a degree which finally made life in this imperfect world unbearable. Here it is the student Vasiliev who cannot, for all his efforts to behave like his cheerful coarse-grained companions, act as they do on a night in the prostitutes' quarter. Chekhov's own feeling about the problem of prostitution is clear from his letter to Suvorin about this story, where he speaks of Sobolev Street in Moscow as 'a regular slave market'. There is more than a question of individual psychology involved then in this story, and as so often before, without any direct pointing of the moral, Chekhov is drawing a contrast between the humane and the inhumane. So also in the longer stories, *A Dreary Story* (1889), *The Duel* (1891) and *Ward No. 6* (1892). In all of these the question which Tolstoy had put so forcibly to the cultivated reader: 'What are we to do?' is inevitably suggested, though Chekhov is showing us in what circumstances people ask themselves this question, and is not himself answering it. In a letter of 1894, he said that he had been deeply influenced by Tolstoy's philosophy for six or seven years of his life, though he had now outgrown it and was sick of all theorising. It was in any case Tolstoy's way of expressing his ideas, and 'a sort of hypnotism' that had affected him, not the ideas themselves, some of which seemed to him to be based on familiar peasant virtues, and others exaggerated and inimical to life.

The period to which Chekhov is referring is no doubt, as we have suggested, the transition years following 1885 or 1886, when a philosophy of life seemed to him what he chiefly needed for his art. Even as late as 1892 a letter to Suvorin describes their age as a great one for science and technics, but not for literature. Good writers have always had a goal towards which they summoned others. Thinking in particular of Tolstoy, he goes on: 'The best of them are realists and paint life as it is, but because every line is steeped in the consciousness of a goal, you feel, besides life as it is, the life which ought to be, and that captivates you. And we? We! We paint life as it is, but beyond that, nothing at all. Flog us and we can do no more! We have neither immediate nor remote aims, and in our soul there is a great empty space. We have no politics, we do not believe in revolutions, we have no God, we are not afraid of ghosts, and I personally am not afraid even of death and blindness. One who wants nothing, hopes for nothing and fears nothing cannot be an artist.'

This despairing cry might also remind us of Hölderlin's 'Und wozu Dichter in dürftiger Zeit' ('Of what use is it to be a poet in an unpropitious age?'), of Mr T. S. Eliot's 'dissociation of consciousness' theory about modern literature and what Professor Heller has called the 'hazard of modern poetry', if it were not so clearly written in a fit of depression, at a time when Chekhov was just throwing off the last effects of Tolstoyanism. It is true that he never ceased to write with rare imaginative insight of priests and monks and bishops, and of the Easter celebrations beloved of all Russians. He had none of the free-thinker's hostility to the church, and felt possibly a half-unconscious nostalgia for its peace, but this outburst is more probably due to the Tolstoyan influence, combined with the insistent demand of the intelligentsia for guidance, for answers to social and philosophical problems, from their favorite writers, and their criticism of Chekhov for only stating problems. But as the 1894 letter already quoted shows, it was not long before Chekhov finally rejected the abstract doctrine of Tolstoy, 'the hedgehog', to use Mr Isaiah Berlin's terminology, his attempt to relate everything in life to a single central truth, a metaphysical belief. Even Tolstoy was by nature, as Mr Berlin has shown, a 'fox', delighting in life's infinite variety. Chekhov was one too, and he was fortunately free from the mental conflict between his nature and his aspirations which tortured Tolstoy. He remained to the end an unrepentant liberal humanist. He firmly rejected the notion of two kinds of truth and was whole-heartedly on the side of science in any conflict with religion. A letter to Dyagilev in 1902, about a philosophical-religious movement for which his support was sought, makes the point quite clear, and in a later letter he says he cannot understand how any intelligent person can be a believer.

In this lack of metaphysical interests Chekhov was clearly a child of the age of naturalism, as in several other respects:

31

his insistence, when he theorised in his letters, on 'absolute truth' to life, including its seamy side, his concern in his stories with the causes, and not least the physical causes, of mental states (*The Party*), also in the social idealism, of which more will be said later. When he tried to formulate his beliefs, they took the shape of a philosophical naturalism, a belief in a full and free natural life. 'Absolute freedom—freedom from violence and insincerity under any form' is what he stressed most of all, and as we have seen, it had taken him some time to acquire the feeling of independence, the capacity to stand on his own feet as a free artist. But as he was too intelligent not to realise the corresponding need for self-discipline, he respected any sincere belief and was capable of reverence. When he described his idea of a cultured man, in an appeal to his bohemian brother Nicolai in 1886, the qualities he represented as most essential were—respect for human personality and consideration for other people's feelings, Christian virtues. His own gentleness and his unselfish work for his family, the village where he settled and innumerable good causes proved that he was no hypocrite.

Before writing *A Dreary Story*, the first of the three important longer stories mentioned above, Chekhov had twice attempted to write a full-length novel, but failed. After the great Russian works of the nineteenth century, the novel was now the supreme literary form. He made a first attempt apparently in 1887, but gave it up after a long struggle, though in the same year he was able to write the play *Ivanov* in a couple of weeks. Then he tried again, having learnt, as he said to Suvorin in 1888, that he must 'train himself to communicate ideas in a narrative form'. He was still misled, most critics would probably now agree, by the belief that 'ideas' capable of logical expression are primary, that a novel must have an 'ideology' behind it. He wanted, he says, 'to paint life faithfully and at the same time to show how that life deviated from the norm', and in addition to his already mentioned difficulty with extended narrative, he found that there was too little system in his ideas. He did not know what the norm was, and could only define it as 'the absolute freedom of man', the liberal humanist ideal. Again he failed to satisfy himself, though it used to be thought that the only stories he published which are connected by a common framework, *The Man in a Case, Gooseberries* and *About Love* (1898), are fragments of the abandoned novel; but notes bearing on them appear so late in his notebooks that this seems unlikely.

The longer stories with which Chekhov in the end contented

himself, though they cannot be described as novels, are all concerned with questions of conscience and intended for a thoughtful reader. He seems to be 'primarily interested not in the soul's relation with other souls', as Virginia Woolf found, to her bewilderment, 'but in the soul's relation to health'. It can be understood that his work now readily found acceptance in the 'fat monthlies' read by the intelligentsia, and a writer who could satisfy their editors had definitely arrived. It is clear that Chekhov was trying out different ways of expanding the sketches of figures in a landscape or other setting in which he had so far excelled. *The Party* had already run to fifty pages, but *The Steppe* (1887) was three times as long. Here Chekhov drew a series of contiguous landscapes, through which the same figure passed on a journey. Turgeniev was no doubt the model, but Chekhov discovered a type of landscape which he thought his predecessors had neglected, the at first sight monotonous expanse of the steppes of southern Russia, which he had re-visited in the previous year and drawn with success in *Happiness*. He was not entirely satisfied with *The Steppe*, agreeing with the criticism that he had produced a series of small pictures on a large canvas. The subject of the story is indeed the steppe it-self in all its moods, seen chiefly through the fresh eyes of a boy of ten, leaving home for the first time to go to a distant school. The boy and the varied figures introduced into the landscape are thoroughly alive; we see earth and sky, birds and insects, as his young eyes see them; we gain a sense of what the steppe has meant in human experience, for the pre-historic builders of the 'kurgany' at one extreme and the sheep farmers and innkeepers of the present at the other. But the landscape dwarfs the human figures, and the chief impression that remains with us is of endlessly varied and ever-changing natural beauty, little heeded by man. Here more than anywhere else Chekhov is found following up the pantheistic nature worship of the Romantics. He never ceased to introduce land-scape backgrounds, as a reminder of the elemental forces that surround us, but he never again made the landscape such a central feature as here.

In the following longer stories, we see him attempting to get away from his accustomed method of presenting his char-acters in 'scenes', and at the same time to deal with serious ideas in fiction. By this time his Tolstoyan ideas were gradually losing their hold on him, and he usually contents himself with the negative aim of 'expressing the longing for a common idea and painfully admitting our need of one.' (P. N. Ostrovsky.)

So in *A Dreary Story* (1889), he gives us the life of a famous scholar, a Russian professor of medicine of international reputation, movingly told by himself as he nears the retiring age and realises more and more clearly the tragic consequences of his inability to share the inner life of those dearest to him. Through his successful concentration on the intellectual life, the springs of human feeling have dried up in him, and at the same time he has lost all conception of 'a common idea, or the God of a living man'. This study of the effect of increasing age and intellectual desiccation, in a world where 'God is dead', gives in ninety pages a surprisingly full picture of contemporary academic life in Russia, through several contrasted figures and the family circle of the professor, with its own peculiar tensions. The central theme is as usual the unbridgeable separateness of the lives of sensitive and intelligent men and women, for whom, however, a self-contained stoical equanimity is represented as being not an ideal, but a kind of living death.

One may discern a turning away from Tolstoy here, but it is clearer in *The Duel* (1891) and *Ward No. 6* (1892). *The Duel* is the longest story of Chekhov's maturity (160 pages), and like *A Dreary Story* and several stories which follow, though it has not the range in time or the multiplicity of figures of a normal novel, it does not strike us as a blown-up short story. The picture of a man and of his whole circle is built up slowly and deliberately, and it produces an effect of completeness. Again the 'hero' is an intellectual, a university graduate who, like the married woman with whom he runs away to the Caucasus, prides himself on his individual freedom. The effect on his character and on his happiness of living for freedom is so catastrophic that the story reads like a criticism of the central idea which Chekhov had earlier proposed for his novel. Even more space than in *A Dreary Story* is taken up by serious talk about the meaning of life. The two leading characters, Laevsky and Von Koren, are made to criticise each other's ideas in long speeches addressed not to each other, for they could not bear that, but to good listeners introduced for the purpose, the good-humoured army doctor and the deacon. Similarly Laevsky's mistress Nadezhda is frankly harangued about her faults by the talkative and self-righteous Maria Constantinovna. Narrative and reported self-examination also take up more space than usual. The situations which make these successive revelations of character and ideas possible, at the doctor's table d'hôte, the picnic and Maria's party, are well contrived, but the main critic of the decadent Laevsky, the zoologist Von Koren, is not

34

much more than a mouthpiece for ideas, while the duel and its surprising result, the conversion of Laevsky, are perhaps a little forced, and the conclusion, that 'in their search for truth men advance two steps and fall back one', like the small boat taking Von Koren out to his ship, is disappointingly vague.

In this story especially, we feel that out of consideration for the public at whom it was directed, the intelligentsia, Chekhov had allowed intellectual ideas too big a part, or rather, the emotional idea which was the starting point had not become flesh, so to speak, as it must in a completely satisfying story or play. An anonymous dramatist has described the process well. There is 'a life and death struggle between the idea and the characters for existence,' he says, at a certain stage in the composition of a play. 'If the idea gains the upper hand, the conception of the whole is doomed. In the successful issue, the idea is . . . "sucked up" by the characters as a sponge sucks up water, until no trace of the idea is left outside the characters.'[1] To vary the metaphor, in *The Duel*, the ideas are in suspension, rather than in solution. It was not unnatural that liberal critics like Merezhkovsky took Von Koren's ideas for Chekhov's own, though he is clearly intended as a dramatic figure, invented to assert in an extreme, almost totalitarian form the claims of society on the individual. The misinterpretation is partly to be ascribed to the fact that the story was printed in the conservative *New Times*, though Chekhov's stories and articles for this paper were in fact unpolitical. He disliked the political views of its editor, Suvorin, but could not afford to neglect the good payment he could offer at a critical time. He also grew to like Suvorin as a man and became a close personal friend of his, until disagreement over the Dreyfus affair separated them.

Ward No. 6 could not be interpreted by anyone as conservative in feeling, and it was fittingly published in the liberal monthly *New Thought*. After this Chekhov ceased to write for the *New Times*, and though he had always to remember the censorship in order to be published at all, the liberal tendency of his thought became more obvious in his stories, and they were felt more and more to express the longings of the age. *Ward No. 6* was, and still is, in Russia, one of the most discussed of Chekhov's stories. It may be taken as the first work of his in which Tolstoyan ideas are unmistakably weighed and found wanting, and the first of his markedly sociological stories. His interest in social problems had been evident, as we saw, from very early,

[1] Quoted by E. Bullough in his article 'Psychical Distance', *British Journal of Psychology*, V (1912), p. 115.

and he had written stories full of social interest, such as *The Cattle Dealers* (1887), *The Bet* and *Lights* (1888), *The Princess* (1889), *The Horse-stealers* (1890), *Peasant Wives* (1891), *The Wife* and *In Exile* (1892). But the symbolism of *Ward No. 6* seemed to convey the oppressive atmosphere of life in Russia in the 'nineties in a profounder and more moving way than any of his earlier stories. Dr Ragin is a very different apostle of culture from Laevsky. He has a real love for sweetness and light—in literature, and spends most of his time reading history and philosophy. But he is the head of a zemstvo hospital, and to throw up his hands and let things take their dreadful course there, as past mending in his generation, comforting himself with the thought that the life of the mind is more important than the relief of suffering, indeed, would be endangered if suffering were too efficiently relieved, is irresponsible escapism. The mental patient whom he finds in ward No. 6 disillusions him. Only those who share the pain of the world have the right to comfort themselves with quotations from Marcus Aurelius, for there is a kind of selfishness in thinking too much of one's own peace of mind.

'When I had read this story to the end,' said Lenin, 'I was filled with awe. I could not remain in my room and went out of doors. I felt as if I were locked up in a ward too.' Ward No. 6, with its helpless inmates, browbeaten by Nikita the porter, was equated by contemporary readers with Russia under Alexander III, according to modern biographers of Chekhov like Derman and Yermilov, who of course tend to exaggerate the social criticism in Chekhov. But his concern at the state of Russia is attested by many witnesses who knew him personally, and we have as further evidence the fact of his visit to Sakhalin Island, the comments in his letters home and the book he wrote about it. It was not the gaolers and superintendents who were to blame for what went on in the Russian prisons, he said, but the Russian people themselves. It was to accomplish what he could as an individual, through his gifts as a writer, that he undertook a journey across Siberia, so hazardous for one in his state of health, in 1890. When he settled for health reasons in the country, at Melikhovo, in 1892, he gave generously of his time and money to heal the sick, to improve the hospitals, to take measures against a threatened epidemic of cholera. He was elected to the zemstvo, became interested in rural education and built three schools at his own expense. It is not surprising that a good half of his stories in this decade are on themes which cannot be considered to be merely individual and family problems, or that long before the 1917 revolution, critics were interpreting his work as saying: 'It is impossible to go on living like this!' According to Bunin, it was the story *Peasants* (1897), published in the advanced monthly *Russian Thought*, which first attracted the attention of a wider public to Chekhov as a social critic. Until then, he says, he had been regarded simply as an entertaining writer, and this is understandable, for although the discussion of social problems is one element in the stories discussed above and in a number of others, *Peasants* is too outspoken for anyone to overlook its challenge to the ordinarily accepted literary view of Russian village life. It was followed up by *The New Villa*, *On Official Duty*, and *In the Ravine*.

Instead of the idealised picture of village innocence and contentment which had been current since the 'Populist' movement, we are shown the 'ignorant insensitive people, always thinking of money, quarreling over a crust of bread, coarse and uncouth in their manners', of whom the deacon in *The Duel* had already spoken. It is a horrifyingly convincing picture of the life of the peasantry, drawn from years of observation by the grandson of a liberated serf. Into earlier stories he had introduced discussions about possible remedies, the upshot of which was that there was none in sight, and that the palliatives administered by the 'conscience-stricken gentry', the young gentlefolk who went out among the people, had done very little good in the end—had perhaps even served to enslave the peasants further by masking the need for more fundamental changes. Yet it was only human nature if individuals like these Populists felt impelled to do what they could (*An Artist's Story*, 1896), though they usually discovered, if they were honest with themselves, that in the hopeless struggle they had done little if anything beyond temporarily salving their own consciences (*My Life*, 1896). And this sensitiveness of conscience was in itself a good thing, perhaps the only ultimate hope for the world, if the idealists did not content themselves with 'a monkishness without self-denial', in the form of the simple life in the country. 'Clearly, the happy man has an easy conscience only because the unhappy bear their burden in silence, and but for this silence his happiness would be impossible. There ought to stand at the door of every self-satisfied happy man someone with a hammer, to remind him continually by his knocking of the existence of unhappy people in the world' (*Gooseberries*, 1898). Suffering is an inescapable element in life, against which it is morally dangerous to be too carefully

moral
soc.

37

cushioned, as the aristocracy tend to be (*The Princess*, 1889).

Among the 'social' stories we may include also two or three which have as their subject the human results of the industrialism which was just beginning to develop in Russia, largely under foreign leadership, and one detailed study of a wholesale merchant's family during two generations: all presented to us, as usual, fictive individual characters, seen from within; but they are also social types with generic features. In *A Woman's Kingdom* (1894), for instance, we see an engineering firm built up by two brothers, whose gifts are complementary to each other, the one supplying the technical skill and insight, without any thought of monetary gain, the other the organising ability, energised by an ascetic love of power. The story asks what an intelligent young woman, inheriting such a show-piece of capitalistic enterprise from her father and uncle, would feel about it all, about the noisy engineering shop, the ill-housed workmen, and her own personal problems, having been brought up very simply and suddenly overwhelmed with wealth. *A Doctor's Visit* (1898) similarly poses a moral problem concerning a big industry, a cotton mill in the country, in which a young doctor from Moscow, who is asked to visit a patient there, finds something which he can only describe as diabolic, in the sights and sounds he encounters, and in the questionable effect of this concentration of power, on society, on those employed there, and even on his patient, the wealthy owner, again a young woman with a conscience.

In the long story *Three Years* (1895), finally, a kind of *Forsyte Saga* in miniature, we see the problem of the generations not in an industrial, but a commercial setting, one which Chekhov knew well from his own youth, though it is a big Moscow firm he shows us, such as his father had worked for in later life. Again the unquestioning self-assertiveness of the father has given place to the religious escapism of one son and the vague fear of life of the other. The development is traced against this background, through the first three years of the younger son's married life, of the emotional relationships of a small group of people, nearly all frustrated in one way or another, and all incurably isolated as individuals. This is how Chekhov continues to see human relationships, in all the stories mentioned and also in some which develop on a larger scale the love stories discussed above, where the setting is of minor importance. Good examples are *The Teacher of Literature* (1894) or Chekhov's last story, *The Betrothed* (1903), in both of which themes rather similar to those of the great plays

Chekhov wrote in these later years are developed with all the resources of his mature art. He could afford now to take his own time over them, he knew his powers and his limitations, he gave free play to his fine sense of form, leaving no trace of the originating idea 'outside the characters' and providing models of artistic construction on which none of his countless imitators have been able to improve.

Summing up his merits as a storyteller, Mirsky says that 'in architectural unity he surpasses all the writers of the realistic age' and is only equalled among Russian writers by Pushkin and Lermontov. Henry James, who found the novels of Tolstoy and Dostoievsky not tasteless indeed, because of the mind and soul in them, but as regards form mere 'fluid puddings', saw in Chekhov's writings not only the imprint of a personality, but also the mark of a master-builder, a feeling for shape and artistic economy which give each work style as a whole as well as in the parts. And Virginia Woolf writes: 'Once the eye is used to these shades, half the "conclusions" of fiction fade into thin air; they show like transparencies with a light behind them—gaudy, glaring, superficial. . . . On the other hand, the method which at first seemed so casual, inconclusive, and occupied with trifles, now appears the result of an exquisitely original and fastidious taste, choosing boldly, arranging infallibly, and controlled by an honesty for which we can find no match save among the Russians themselves.'

III

The Playwright

We have noticed in Chekhov's stories his fondness for what we have called 'scenes', where his talent for lively dialogue is evident, and for plots resembling French classical drama in their treatment of time. In his plays we are constantly being reminded of the characteristics of both the man and the artist which we have found in the stories. Even as a schoolboy he had tried his hand at writing plays; he never lost his early interest in the stage and in actors and actresses as human beings. It is not surprising that, in spite of disappointments, he made repeated attempts as a dramatist from his first years in Moscow and, when he had found a technique which satisfied him, devoted the last decade of his life principally to the theatre. Now that his art as a story-teller has lost some of its novelty for us

39

through the lapse of time and through the successful imitation of his methods, it is probably as a dramatist that he is most widely known and appreciated, at least abroad, for in this field he has remained inimitable.

Among Chekhov's plays, as among his stories, we have to distinguish a group of short humorous works, written quite frankly for money and little known outside Russia, from the serious longer works into which he put the best that was in him. The vaudevilles were written quickly, to please their own particular public, and though they have no particular literary pretensions they are technically excellent, full of comic invention, ingenious, lively dialogue and dramatically effective surprises. They quickly earned and they have retained great popularity on the Russian stage. As it is almost impossible to convey in a translation an adequate impression of their peculiarly Russian atmosphere and racy speech, their humour often sounds a little elementary to foreigners, though *The Bear, The Proposal, The Wedding, The Anniversary*, all written between 1888 and 1891, have been acted in England with success.

Chekhov's first surviving attempt at a serious play was never acted, and published only after his death, because he soon came to see that its faults were incurable. It is a very interesting document for admirers of his later work and was therefore translated, and slightly adapted, by Basil Ashmore in 1952, under the title *Don Juan (in the Russian Manner)*. It is too long and complicated, it follows too closely the already old-fashioned Russian technique of the early 'eighties, but it possesses unmistakably the same bitter-sweet flavour as the most characteristic of the stories, the same preference for characters under the stress of unfulfilled desires, in the enervating conditions of everyday provincial life in Russia. No less than five love intrigues, half pathetic, half farcical, are the result of Platonov's irresistible though unsought power to charm the ladies of a small town, to escape whom his only refuge in the end is suicide. It is a kind of *Werther* in reverse. Several characters give the impression of being first drafts of those we find in the mature plays, and the general tone of the dialogue, as well as what Desmond McCarthy calls the 'ingeniously haphazard methods of revealing human nature', are already thoroughly Chekhovian.

Platonov himself, in particular, has much in common with the 'hero' of the first serious play of Chekhov's that was acted, *Ivanov* (1887). The theme is the inevitable fading of youth's generous ideals with the passing of the years, expressed long before this in Faust's lines:

40

> The feelings which were then our very life
> Are stifled in the turmoil of the world,

or as Platonov puts it, referring to this same liberal humanism which had been the inspiration of the Russian intelligentsia, 'When one is young it's all so simple. On the one side, Shakespeare, Beethoven and Goethe . . . on the other, money, vanity and decadence.' *Ivanov* depicts the last stages in the disillusionment of a 'man of the 'sixties', a liberal of that era which initiated the so-called 'great reforms' and the democratic zemstvo movement. Ivanov is a landowner, whose youthful ideals had turned sour on him at thirty, and who at thirty-five finds life completely unbearable. What we actually see is only the unhappy final stage of his career, the play being constructed on the 'analytic' plan, with 'scenes' also conceived in accordance with the French convention, that the entrance or exit of a character, without any change of place, constitutes a new scene. Very little happens outwardly in the course of the play. Ivanov, depressed by his failures, bored with his adoring but delicate wife, worried by the thought of the money he owes to the rich but miserly wife of a neighbour, among others, spends his evenings at this neighbour's hospitable house, where the young daughter, Sasha, thinks Ivanov a remarkable man, whose happiness she could still restore. At the end of the second act, when she has just of her own accord declared her love for him, his wife enters as they are embracing. Sasha visits him at home when, after this, he tries to avoid her, annoying him and reducing his wife to despair. A year after his wife has died of consumption, and of sorrow at his neglect, the persistent Sasha has brought him to the verge of marriage, but at the last moment, when the wedding guests have already arrived, he realises how he has been deceiving himself in thinking that at his age life can begin afresh, and shoots himself.

The play is a study of an age and a milieu as much as of a character. Ivanov holds an office (that of 'permanent member of the committee for peasant affairs') which was abolished in 1889, and he and the village intelligentsia, who with their wives and friends account for most of the characters of the play, all show signs of the resignation from exhaustion which followed the age of the great reforms. It was a new subject for the theatre, and Chekhov spared no pains to make the play a work of literary as well as theatrical significance, by avoiding the stereotyped both in content and form. Though for our modern taste it seems not startlingly novel but rather the reverse, the actors found it so difficult that Chekhov had to write long explanatory letters to even the best of them. They expected, following the accepted tradition, to be able to take sides with the 'hero', but Chekhov, aiming at truth to the life of his time, put in the centre of his play a man who could be neither whole-heartedly admired nor completely despised, a tired, confused and unsuccessful reformer, with the 'beautiful past' behind him which Chekhov considered typical for the intelligent Russian gentleman of that day. The liberal gentry, in Chekhov's view, in spite of all their good intentions, usually got themselves involved in unnecessary difficulties through their reforming zeal, and quickly lost heart. In the story *Neighbours* (1892) he drew a landowner who married, out of pity, a girl seduced by a fellow-officer, and soon found her too much for him. He is full of liberal commonplaces but completely incapable of running his estate. Ivanov is a better specimen of a similar type, a man who, fresh from the university, married a Jewess, took up land-reform and zemstvo work with enthusiasm and at the age of thirty is already beginning to feel bored and jaded. He cannot find the causes for his failure in the external world, and he has no intelligent neighbours to advise him. Looking within, he finds only that very Russian feeling, an indefinite sense of guilt. This is how Chekhov himself analyses his character in the letters.

In the opening scenes of the play we hear one after another of those around Ivanov offering him their unacceptable remedies. It is an exposition remarkable for the skill with which Chekhov conveys an atmosphere, the indefinite mood of boredom and longing that broods over Ivanov's country house. As in the stories he had used landscape to reinforce the emotional effect, so here he uses sights and sounds to orchestrate the dialogue. It is dusk, a lamp is burning on the table on the terrace where Ivanov is sitting, and from time to time, in a pause in the dialogue, an owl's melancholy cry is heard or the watchman's rattle as he makes his rounds or, for contrast, a cheerful folksong from the kitchen quarters. It is an owl's nest of a house, as the doctor says. The characters think aloud in monologues; even when speaking to others they often characterise themselves by their self-analysis, but Ivanov is also discussed by each of the others and presented to us through the distorting mirror of their individual temperaments. Each separate view of Ivanov is psychologically understandable in the speaker and helps to characterise him too, but no one gives us the absolute truth about Ivanov as the author sees it. We are left to form our own conclusions about him, and many of the first readers and spectators wrongly took the self-righteous young Doctor Lvov, with his ethical principles based on conscious reasoning from clear ideas, as the author's mouthpiece, much as Von Koren in *The Duel* was misunderstood later. Lvov is a prig, completely lacking in intuitive sympathy, and his explanation of Ivanov's conduct from motives of narrow self-interest, even though it is shared by the cynical older members of the Lebedev circle, in a neighbouring mansion, is just as false as Sasha Lebedev's admiration of Ivanov as a personality is extravagant, and her motives for wishing to 'save' him ambiguous. The only wholly likeable character in the play is Ivanov's wife, who has lost his affection for no cause he can analyse, and certainly not because her wealthy parents have disappointed him of the dowry he expected. It is not surprising that audiences and readers had difficulty in appreciating a drama of everyday life which is built up on the principle, of which we found the first example in the Platonov play, that all the leading characters shall find themselves frustrated in their deeper purposes. Yet this new dramatic convention is a further symbolic illustration of the view of life so often suggested, as we have seen, in the stories, with their insistence on the slight hold that our values have on actual existence.

The ideal of drama which Chekhov no doubt already had at the back of his mind was the psychological naturalism which he brought to perfection in his later plays, a drama which should be content to make the spectator fully aware of complicated states of mind in a group of invented characters, without asking whether the result fitted in with any accepted notions about comedy or tragedy, so long as it interpreted convincingly the general sense of life as we know it. But in *Ivanov* Chekhov still follows the melodramatic tradition of his day in working up to strong act-endings. To end a play, he once complained, no one has ever invented any alternatives to a marriage or a pistol-shot. Here he chose the latter, not for the last time. What really interests him, however, is not the explicit action in the play so much as the lifelike presentation of character in dialogue and everyday incidents. He gives us a small number of characters in the round besides Ivanov, characters which do not develop in the course of the play, but reveal their complex but unchanging natures more fully in each successive scene. They are surrounded by a large number of 'flat' characters presented as types, with 'Leitmotiv' mannerisms and sayings of their own, which make them immediately recognisable—the doctor's insistence on honesty, the estate manager's clowning and absurd

43

projects, the count's cynical marriage plans, the stinginess of the neighbour's wife, her husband's fondness for the bottle and the excise officer's tiresome talk of cards. The chief characters generally speak the normalised Russian of the intelligentsia, but the minor characters, especially the uneducated ones, are often given their own peculiar idiom, as in the stories. Chekhov had already perfected a method of presenting character in dialogue which he did not need to change later. Dramatic silences are used, sometimes to retard the tempo, sometimes, broken by noises off, to create an atmosphere, sometimes merely to mark a change of theme in the conversation; and again and again the obstinate separateness of the individual is emphasised, by his deafness to what others are saying and his persistence in thinking his own thoughts aloud.

Encouraged by the success of *Ivanov* when performed in St Petersburg, and the lively discussions which followed, Chekhov tried to get still further away from the conventional play constructed along a thin thread of plot, still closer to the unemphatic casual dialogue of everyday life, in the play he called *The Wood Demon* (1889). It was put on in Moscow and failed to please, and it was rejected by the Imperial Theatres in St Petersburg, so Chekhov laid it aside until seven years later he made out of it his *Uncle Vanya*. He had written it quickly, after pondering for some time over the theme, and he felt himself, when it was finished, that in this 'comedy-novel' he had not paid enough attention to the requirements of the stage, in his attempt to bring the drama nearer to the novel. It had become something of 'a mosaic', with 'a prevailing tone of pure lyricism'. For the next few years, disappointed also, as we have seen, in his experiments with the novel, he devoted all his energies to the great series of his longer stories, only returning to the theatre, apart from occasional farces, with *The Seagull*, in 1895.

The Seagull displays the same tendencies as *The Wood Demon*, and though it was better thought out and better adapted to stage performance, this play too, to his intense disappointment, was a complete failure when first produced, at the Alexandrovsky Theatre in St Petersburg, in October 1896. It was badly acted, partly because its form was altogether too novel for the ordinary actor, as well as for the playgoer. 'The action of the play,' Suvorin wrote in his diary, 'takes place behind the scenes rather than on the stage, as though its author was only interested in showing how his characters reacted to events, to reveal their natures.' For Suvorin, a dramatist of sorts himself, a play was not a play unless it was full of 'dramatic' action in the traditional sense. Similarly the theatre manager Korsch, at the first reading rehearsal, had criticised Chekhov for making Treplev shoot himself off stage, without even making a speech first. In banishing violent action from the stage Chekhov was, of course, only coming further into line with the classical tradition, which he had followed already in adopting an analytic type of construction, and the leading European dramatists of the 'nineties, Ibsen, Hauptmann and Maeterlinck, had provided many new examples of a drama concerned above all with the inner life. Chekhov had clearly found something to learn from Ibsen, both in his social and in his poetic plays, though he said he did not really like him. Hauptmann's so deceptively casual conversation scenes and Maeterlinck's use of symbolism had also given him new ideas. There are many features in *The Seagull*, as in the stories, which seem to belong to a subtle, psychological type of naturalism. Chekhov goes to unprecedented lengths in the apparent haphazardness of the dialogue, rarely developing any theme fully but presenting many themes in intermingled fragments, to the accompaniment of trivial everyday actions. His characters amuse themselves with amateur theatricals, they read aloud to each other, play lotto and talk about their health, and all the time the setting never changes within the act, there are no separate numbered scenes in the printed play, and people seem to drift in and out as the spirit moves them.

Yet the general effect of the play is not naturalistic at all but profoundly poetical, lyrical in a dramatic way, in the sense that Chekhov does not express through the characters his own personal feeling, but seems to make the emotional life of a small group of people transparent for us, universalised, and therefore profoundly moving, as he does in his stories. We get to know what they feel not just about particular people in particular situations, but about life in general. The strong undercurrents of emotion which determine, more than any changing circumstances, their everyday moods become visible—deep, irrational longings, regrets, enthusiasms and above all, love, a love whose object is almost always unattainable.

'Why do you always go about in black?' Medvedenko, the village school-teacher, asks Masha, the daughter of the estate-manager Shamraev, at the beginning of *The Seagull*. 'It is mourning for my life. I am unhappy,' she replies, and this expression of self-pity evokes from Medvedenko, who loves her but is merely tolerated by her, the characteristic reflection which becomes his Leitmotiv: 'Why? I can't understand you . . .

45

You are healthy, your father and mother are perhaps not well off, but quite comfortable. My life is much harder than yours. I get 23 roubles a month all told, and they take some of that for my pension, and yet I don't wear mourning.' The self-revelation is interrupted by a reference to the imminent performance, by Treplev and a young girl from a neighbouring estate, Nina, of Treplev's play, then Masha takes snuff and talks about the weather before saying: 'You are always philosophising or talking about money ... but I think it is a thousand times easier to go about in rags and beg than ...' There she breaks off, conveying to the audience a hint of two levels of thought, one she can speak out to Medvedenko, and one which she cannot, for it would wound him and is half a secret, the thought of her own unhappy love, for Treplev, as we soon see. The occupation of the moment, social talk and deeper feeling are all elements in the consciousness that is so unobtrusively revealed to us. Gradually others are added to the group, Sorin, the proprietor of the estate, a retired civil servant, always longing to be back in town, and his nephew Treplev, a young man with literary ambitions. We have been told a little about Treplev before he appears, and now we are similarly prepared by Sorin and Treplev, while they are revealing themselves to us with every word, for the appearance of Sorin's sister Arkadina, a famous actress. Meanwhile Masha and her admirer have been asked to go away until the play begins, for which preparations are still going on behind the curtain of the improvised open-air theatre. A remark about his unkempt appearance evokes from Sorin the words: 'I was never liked by women,' and then, after a pause, as they sit down, 'Why is my sister in a bad temper?' 'Oh, she's bored,' Treplev replies. 'And she is jealous. She is already against me, and against the idea of this performance, and against my play, because Nina is acting and she is not. She hasn't read my play, but she already detests it.' So the exposition goes on. We hear from Treplev about his mother's vanity and close-fistedness, her out-of-date notions about the theatre and her passion for the writer Trigorin. We hear about his own love for Nina, about the new forms he thinks the theatre needs, about his personal difficulties with such a mother and about the successes of Trigorin. Sorin breaks in again with: 'But I like literary men, you know. Once upon a time there were just two things I passionately wanted, to get married and to be a writer, but I haven't pulled off either.'

Nina arrives just in time for the play, which must open as the moon is rising, and while Sorin is sent to call the others, she too tells us about herself: 'My father and step mother won't let me come here. They say it is too bohemian ... They are afraid I might go on the stage ... But I am drawn to this lake like a seagull ... My heart is full of you all.' They kiss and talk about future meetings, so difficult because of her parents. Nina is excited at the thought of meeting Treplev's mother and above all, the great Trigorin. At last the full audience is assembled for the play within the play, which, we have been told, will be in a new form, and rather remote from ordinary life. The talk is of the theatre. As they take their seats, Arkadina mockingly quotes the queen in Hamlet, reminding us of another play within a play, and Treplev caps the quotation with lines which bring out the tension between this mother and her son. When the curtain goes up and we have heard part of Nina's opening monologue as the World Spirit, twenty thousand years from now, reflecting on the disppearance of all life from the earth, we are not surprised at Arkadina's impatient dismissal of the play as 'some sort of decadent stuff' or, soon after, at Treplev's angry order to lower the curtain. He leaves them in disgust to discuss the play, to pay compliments to Nina, and, when singing is heard from across the lake, to recall the gay times that these lakeside estates have known. Nina, until she must hurry home, cannot take her eyes off Trigorin.

Writing to Suvorin about his play, Chekhov had told him he would find in it 'Landscape (a view of a lake), a lot of talk about literature, little action and five poods of love.' The landscape setting plays much the same part as in the stories. It includes not only the stage picture, but all that is suggested by the references in the dialogue to external nature, in response perhaps to sounds that we are made to hear, like the music across the water. The owl's cry in Ivanov had been used in the same way. It all hints at 'the human mass out of which the characters have come, the atmosphere and background'. At the same time it seems to help us to hold the everyday elements in the play at an aesthetic distance, to bathe them in 'the light that never was on sea or land'. Even the fragment of Treplev's play contributes something towards displaying this human scene in the light of eternity, as a poet's dream. The lyricism is thus intensified, and the sadness of frustrated love made bearable and even beautiful.

If we ask why love is always unhappy in Chekhov, one answer that might be suggested is that, like so many artists, he finds happiness undramatic, unproductive of tension. With this autumnal colouring he can achieve original effects. Biographical and sociological explanations might also be found

47

for his preference for it, but they would not account for what he does with it. It belongs to his characteristic palette and like a good painter, he performs wonders within the limitations he imposes on himself, the unity of tone being unmistakable, in spite of what has been called the 'fragmentation' of his themes. The emotional effect of the first act of *The Seagull* is strikingly epitomised in the last speech of Dr Dorn, the middle-aged amorist, when Masha, who in an earlier version was explicitly described as his daughter, has confided to him her secret, her hopeless love for Treplev: 'How highly strung you all are, how highly strung! And what oceans of love . . . Oh magical lake! But what can I do, my child, what can I do?' The lake becomes a symbol for the lure of love and beauty, for what we treasure in life the more because we know it to be fleeting. Nina is drawn to it 'like a seagull'. In the following acts this symbol recurs in several variations, but always with the suggestion of a fragile, 'butterfly beauty' like that of the girl in the story *The Beauties*, or like the 'fruit trees in blossom', a symbol Chekhov was to use later, which for Simone Weil evokes the Greek idea of the divorce between value and existence, the essence of the tragic.

In Act I Treplev is in the centre of the picture, and Chekhov allows him two or three long speeches in which to reveal himself fully to us. In Act II, Trigorin is given a similar opportunity, after the distraught Treplev has laid at Nina's feet a seagull that he has wantonly shot, for him the image of their shattered love. Trigorin is a finished portrait of a professional author, the slave of his profession, with no time and little genuine feeling left for living. The dead seagull and the living Nina, who is irresistibly drawn to him, suggest to him a subject for a short story. 'On the shore of a lake a girl has lived from childhood, like you; she loves the lake, as a seagull might, and she is happy and free like a seagull. But a man happens to come along and see her, and having nothing better to do he destroys her, as this seagull has been destroyed.'

The symbol is woven into the plot in such a way that it almost serves the purpose of the oracle in Greek drama, foreshadowing the coming action, for in between the acts Treplev tries, unsuccessfully, to take his own life as he had said he would, and in Act III Nina offers herself to Trigorin, using the same device, we are told by Lydia Avilov in her reminiscences of Chekhov, as she herself had used with Chekhov in 1895, a message conveyed by a reference to one of his stories by page and line, engraved on a pendant for a watch-chain. Chekhov did not respond, and in fact the whole story of Mme Avilov's love for him is clearly very subjectively told by her and throws little light on his work. But Trigorin in the play duly ruins Nina in the interval of two years which we have to imagine before Act IV opens, again at Sorin's house by the lake. The background action of everyday comings and goings has continued all through in what is actually brought before us, the reading aloud and the disputes about carriage horses in Act II, the bandaging of Treplev and the departure to the station in Act III, and in Act IV the game of lotto, in the midst of which Trigorin is reminded by Shamraev of the seagull which he had left to be stuffed. 'I don't remember,' he says, and he repeats the phrase twice after supper, when the stuffed bird is shown to him. The remark has an effect akin to tragic irony. Meanwhile we have heard from Treplev the unfortunate girl's story, and the scene when she calls to see him again has shown us that though Trigorin has left her for his old attachment, and she still cannot accept Treplev's love, she has at last found her feet in the theatre and will have her art to live for, whereas Treplev has to admit failure in what he had thought to be his vocation, writing. Disappointed in his love and in his work he shoots himself, off stage, just as Trigorin has denied for the third time any remembrance of the seagull, and Dr Dorn tries to persuade Arkadina, while the game of lotto proceeds, that the bang has been caused by a bursting ether bottle in his medical kit. Again a pistolshot has to provide the conventional ending, but our real interest is not in the final outcome of a single line of action, but in the tangle of relationships between the members of this house-party of excitable intellectuals, as they work themselves out in perfectly ordinary circumstances according to the laws of human nature, yet in a pattern and with a tragic inevitability which remind us in more than one way of Greek tragedy.

Uncle Vanya

The revised version of *The Wood Demon* was finished before the first performance of *The Seagull*, and is clearly by the same hand. It proved surprisingly popular in provincial Russian theatres, after its publication in the collection of Chekhov plays which appeared in 1897. It was given the title *Uncle Vanya* and styled 'Scenes from country life', instead of 'comedy', though there is more of the comic in it than in *The Seagull*, in the secondary characters like Telegin and Marina. The influence of prevailing economic and social conditions on everyday life in the country is strongly stressed, whereas in *The Wood*

Demon, written in Chekhov's Tolstoyan period, it was the personal defects of the characters which were the root cause of their unhappiness. There the 'nest of the intelligentsia', the professor's country house, was seen by its new mistress, his second wife, to be full of hatred and malice, and as in the story *The Duel*, a sudden shock, Uncle Vanya's suicide after a quarrel with his brother-in-law, the professor, brought everyone to their senses. In the final version, deeper causes are made responsible for the 'Heartbreak House' atmosphere. Country life itself, boring, stupid and sordid as it is in Russia, drags intelligent, decent people like Uncle Vanya and the zemstvo doctor Astrov down towards the level of the hard-drinking, inefficient landowners around them. A change of heart would not be enough, Astrov thinks, to bring about an improvement. Society as a whole needs to be remoulded, and the intelligentsia are not equal to the task. For lack of forethought by the governing class, 'thousands of trees perish, the homes of wild creatures are turned into a wilderness, the rivers grow shallow and dry up, glorious landscapes vanish for ever.'

Astrov, with his passion for forestry, is not to be regarded merely as an eccentric. Similar views find expression in Chekhov's tales, and he was himself an enthusiastic treeplanter. Literary and artistic culture, such as the 'nests of the gentry' represent at their best, are not enough to save the world, or even the souls of their devotees. Professor Serebryakov is revealed as a hardened old egoist, who calls on everyone around him for sacrifices in the name of learning but is himself a sham, producing nothing of real value to the world. For twenty years Uncle Vanya has managed for a nominal salary the estate which his sister, the Professor's first wife, had inherited, with her mother and brother, and the profits have been sent to the learned man of whom they are all so proud. But now Vanya is disillusioned, partly because the sight of the beautiful second wife of the professor, Elena ('Helena'), reminds him of all he has missed in life. When the professor produces his entirely selfish plan of selling the estate, the half demented Vanya, in this version, shoots at him, but fortunately misses, and here the violent action takes place, for once, on the stage.

The earlier 'comedy' had ended appropriately with two engagements, but that was too conventional for Chekhov's mature taste, so Sonia, the professor's daughter by his first wife, does not here attract Dr Astrov, whom she loves. Chekhov makes Astrov now fall in love, like Vanya, with Elena, complicating the central emotional tangle in the familiar way and providing

50

for a new and striking scene in Act III, in which Elena, not
without unavowed motives of her own, as Astrov sees, acts on
her own suggestion as a go-between, and asks him whether
he can return Sonia's love. By so doing she learns that she
herself is in love with him, and he with her, but she remains
faithful to her gouty old tyrant, mainly perhaps because of
the inertia and lack of energy, reminding one of Goncharov's
Oblomov, in which Astrov sees her chief characteristic and
that of the society around her. A not entirely convincing final
scene shows us Vanya and Sonia resigning themselves again
to their monotonous but useful task of managing the estate,
Vanya to find an anodyne in merely being kept busy, Sonia,
as a believer, in the confident anticipation of a life beyond the
grave in which they will at last find peace. It is difficult to accept
the current Russian interpretation of this ending as courageously
optimistic. The truth seems to be that Chekhov, as we have already seen, often had trouble with his endings, because his
strength lay in the presentation of processes and problems, and
not of solutions. But though this new aspect of Sonia's character seems to be sprung on us too suddenly, and that by
a confessedly agnostic author, for her dreams to sound quite
convincing, the ideal she proclaims of disinterested labour for
others made a strong appeal to many progressive Russians of
the 'nineties, for whom at least the *word* 'work' had the value
of a charm.

The Three Sisters

'Work' is still more a keynote in the next play, *The Three
Sisters*, produced after an interval of four years, when the great
success of *The Seagull* in the first season of the Moscow Art
Theatre (1898), and of *Uncle Vanya* in the provinces, had
restored Chekhov's self-confidence. The theme is again the
passing of time and opportunity unused, the tragic waste of
the best in life, illustrated this time from the life of a family
of three sisters and a brother, children of a general in a provincial capital, who had passed their early years in Moscow. The
play opens a year after their father's death, again with a birthday ('nameday') party, as in *The Wood Demon*, where all the
characters can be introduced. In *Ivanov* a year elapses between
the third and fourth acts, in *The Seagull* two, and in *The Three
Sisters* Chekhov abandons the analytic technique still further
and allows the action to extend over four or five years, his point
being to underline the almost imperceptible but relentless
influence of time. In act I Andrei proposes to Natasha, in Act

II they have a boy a few months old, and in Act III a little girl as well, who in Act IV is beginning to talk. The central characters are accordingly made to develop, instead of remaining fixed, as in *Ivanov*, but the secondary characters are still 'flat' and unchanging, marked by standing phrases and set habits: Dr Chebutykin's newspaper reading, Soleny's posing as a second Lermontov, and so on. The time of day and the season are chosen for their symbolic fitness. When the sisters' hopes of returning to Moscow are still high, in Act I, it is a sunny morning in May, but it is autumn in Act IV, and the geese are migrating, when the garrison departs and Tuzenbach is killed. It is in the small hours of the morning, in Act III, that the characters are most given to philosophising about the meaning of life. Again the beauty of nature is contrasted with what men make of their lives. 'What beautiful trees,' the doomed Tuzenbach cries in Act IV, 'and how beautiful life ought to be in sight of them!'—the trees which Natasha is determined to cut down as soon as she has the house to herself. Other less obvious symbolism increases the lyrical effect of the play: Masha's black dress, her repetition of haunting mysterious lines from Pushkin, Chebutykin's breaking of the porcelain clock and the music heard off stage at various points, particularly of course the gay marches played by the military band, growing fainter and fainter in the distance at the close of the play. The incidents we see and the conversation we hear on the stage are as usual those of everyday life, with family or religious festivals or typical incidents of town life to serve as a focus of attention, the birthday party in the first act, 'Butter Week' in the second, a big fire in the third and the withdrawal of the garrison in the fourth. There is again much self-characterisation, and the characters talk past each other, bent on self-expression more than on communication, the most striking example being Andrei's open confession of his disappointed hopes in Act II, when he knows that the deaf Ferapont cannot hear.

As in *Ivanov* and *Uncle Vanya*, what happens in the play is that something in the atmosphere of Russian provincial life seems to settle like a blight on the souls of people full of promise and bring a drab monotony into their lives. Its effect is most obvious on Andrei, the young man marked out, his sisters thought, for a scholar, who resigns himself prematurely with his Natasha, the essence of petty bourgeois meanness and vulgarity, to the life of a provincial minor official, deceived and bullied by his wife, irresponsibly gambling away his own and his sisters' patrimony and, like Treplev in *The Seagull*, finding only in solitary music an outlet for his despair. But his unmarried sisters too, though sensitive and cultured, and full at first of a naive enthusiasm for useful work, find less and less satisfaction in their occupations as the years go by, and their coarse-grained sister-in-law gradually drives them out of their home, while the dream which had all along consoled them, of returning to Moscow, the promised land of their early memories, is seen to be more and more impossible of fulfilment. Only Masha, married to a comically self-satisfied schoolmaster, finds a passing happiness in her love for Colonel Vershinin, another victim of marriage, until he and the battery he commands are moved elsewhere, taking with them all that had made provincial life tolerable.

The chief characters in *The Three Sisters*, though they would have been called 'intelligentsia' in the broad Russian sense, are not writers, scholars, actors and so on, but ordinary middle-class people of a certain education, and undistinguished officers and officials. Their problems are not those of the exceptionally gifted and sensitive, and though they do seem to be typical Russians of the 'nineties, the play in some ways has a greater universality of appeal than has *Uncle Vanya* or *The Seagull*. Its themes are such things as the freshness of youth and its fading, happy memories of childhood and the longing to return to its scenes, the love of kindred souls bound by inescapable earlier ties, the first flush of joy in useful work, and later doubts of one's vocation—in a word, the plight of us all, who 'look before and after, and pine for what is not'. Here again Soviet criticism dwells on what it calls the optimism of the play, Chekhov's vision of humanity's triumphs to come. Vershinin certainly is often given lines full of similar hopes for the future to those which Chekhov himself sometimes expressed in his later years to friends, and which he introduced into his last story, *The Bride*. 'In two or three hundred years,' Vershinin says, 'life will be unimaginably beautiful,' if his generation and many to come will be content to work self-sacrificingly for the good of their distant descendants. We should note, however, that Andrei too comforts himself with rosy pictures of the future, and he is surely not to be taken for a prophet. Instead of having 'a beautiful past', as in Ivanov's day, it seems as if some Russians were beginning to have a 'beautiful future' with which to console themselves. What has in fact turned out to be prophetic in the play is Tuzenbach's vision of the 'wholesome storm' which would soon sweep away Russian lethargy and indifference, so that in 25 or 30 years it would not be exceptional for Russians to work, but the normal rule. This is naturally taken as a prophecy of the 1917 Revolution, though Chekhov to the end does not seem to have thought a revolution either possible or desirable.

The Cherry Orchard

Chekhov's last play (written in 1903) can be dated from its contents without much difficulty. The action takes place again in a country house, but in a Russia where there are telegraph poles along the main roads—the heroine is constantly receiving wires from her lover in Paris—where maids are beginning to dress like their mistresses, possess watches, powder their noses and make play with their delicate nerves, estate clerks talk an incomprehensible 'educated' language and impudent, much travelled lackeys feel themselves far above their station in life. The isolation of the country is breaking down. There are no motor cars or buses, but the train service to the nearest town is good enough for people to be able to go in for lunch in a restaurant, and week-end cottages are in very great demand. It is possible for the able and energetic son of a village shopkeeper, without much education, to make a fortune in business, and in certain areas fairly near large towns agrarian Russia is fast coming under the influence of modern capitalism, a development particularly favoured by Count Witte's government at the time when the play was written. But the prospectors whose discovery of 'some sort of white clay' on Simeonov-Pishchik's estate makes him, so surprisingly, completely solvent in the last act, after we have seen him in the first three continually touting all his friends for contributions towards the interest on his loans, are still foreigners, Englishmen.

In this new world people like Pishchik, and his neighbours the Ranevskys, are out of their depth. Mme Ranevsky goes on spending recklessly, giving gold to beggars if she has no coppers, buying a villa in Mentone by mortgaging her Russian estate, and so forth, until she reaches the stage when she cannot pay even the interest on what she owes, and must come home to see what can be done about it. That is the opening situation of the play, when her party arrives at the old family mansion after two o'clock in the morning, the train having been two hours late. By this timing, Chekhov not only reminds us of the shortcomings of the railways but emphasises the topsy-turvy and chaotic nature of the family's affairs and provides himself with many unusual and amusing situations from ordinary life. Lopakhin, the shopkeeper's son who has risen in the world, is there to welcome them, and the central theme is quickly made

54

apparent. How will the family satisfy its creditors? Can the sale of the estate be avoided, and what do they all feel about it?

The remaining acts follow in fairly quick succession, so that this play, unlike *The Three Sisters*, is more or less analytic in its construction, the picture of a crisis, the end of a long story. Chekhov changes the scene, however, between the acts, and the debate on the momentous question of what is to be done is continued on a garden bench by the roadside. It is varied by several secondary encounters, which enrich the picture and produce the usual impression of everyday conversation overheard, in the talk between the maid Dunyasha, her old love, the clerk, and his flighty rival, the young lackey, and again between the ever-practical Lopakhin and the 'eternal student' Trofimov, formerly tutor in the family, who is full of abstract ideals and the gospel of progress through science and hard work. Anya, the seventeen-year-old daughter of Mme Ranevsky, thinks him wonderful, and as she makes for the river bank with him in the moonlight, Varya, the serious-minded adopted daughter who looks after the household, calls out her name into the night in vain. In the third act, a farewell party is being given by Mme Ranevsky, while she awaits from town news of the outcome of the auction of her estate. The Jewish orchestra heard in the distance in Act II is now playing dance music ('mention a gun and you must make it go off later!'), gay tunes that contrast with the sad thoughts of the leading characters, as in *The Three Sisters*. The guests are not, as in the old times, generals, barons, admirals. The postmaster and the station master have been invited, and the estate clerk and Dunyasha are dancing with the rest. Deaf old Firs, a survival from the days of serfdom, who had chosen to stay on at the time of the great 'misfortune', as he calls the Emancipation, bores the young lackey with his comments on the change. Anya's German governess, a farcically fantastic creation, performs conjuring tricks and Mme Ranevsky, her nerves on edge, twits Trofimov unmercifully on his claim to be 'above love'—a passage that should be remembered when one is tempted to take Trofimov for Chekhov's mouthpiece. Like Dr Ragin in *Ward No. 6*, he is a shade too ethereal, for Chekhov a sign of weakness. Mme Ranevsky herself sadly reflects that she is 'lower than love', its helpless victim. At last her brother and Lopakhin arrive, and Lopakhin has his moment of triumph. The serf's son has bought the manor house and estate where his father and grandfather would not have been allowed into the kitchen.

In Act IV we again see a family departing for the station.

55

Lopakhin's champagne is left untouched, except by the young lackey. The minor intrigues are neatly wound up. The idealist Trofimov and the hardheaded, hardworking Lopakhin, representing different aspects of the new Russia, part good friends, and Varya does not receive the long-expected proposal from Lopakhin. The scene where they talk about trains and the weather is a masterpiece of indirect expression. The feelings of the Ranevskys at leaving their old home for ever are conveyed to us with a similar subtlety. Mme Ranevsky is allowed a word or two, but her brother, who has been shown to be much given to rhetorical speeches, even addressed to old pieces of furniture, is quickly silenced by his niece, so that the expression of natural sentiment produces at the same time comic relief. But of course the pain they all feel so deeply does not leave us unmoved. On the contrary, it is with us throughout, from their first rapture at seeing again their old nursery, and through the window the magnificent cherry-orchard in bloom, the one thing, beautiful but of very little use, which makes their estate remarkable, to the close of the play, when, through the negligence of the young lackey, old Firs, a dying man, is left alone in the empty mansion, like a captain going down with his ship. It is because old associations prevent them from taking seriously Lopakhin's plan for retrieving their financial position, by laying out the estate in building plots for week-end cottages, that they hesitate and do nothing effective, so that the estate has to be sold over their heads, and as they leave, the sound of the workmen's axes is heard as they fell the trees. The dispute over the cherry-orchard is symbolic not only of the difference between landowners and businessmen, and the older and the younger generation—for Trofimov and Anya look forward to the ideal of making all Russia their garden, in the wonderful new life which is coming—but also of the final variation on what we have found to be a central theme in Chekhov's writings, the fate of beauty on earth, and its preciousness nevertheless to those who put good states of mind higher than the enjoyment of material prosperity.

This is on the whole a comedy of manners rather than of character. Only Mme Ranevsky has the complexity of the characters in Chekhov's serious plays. Even Trofimov and Lopakhin are shown only from one side, as is natural and effective in a comedy. Mme Ranevsky's billiard-playing brother Gaev, the impoverished squire Simeonov-Pishchik and all the servants are caricatured in the manner familiar from Chekhov's farces. He insisted that *The Cherry Orchard* was a vaudeville, and was annoyed with the Moscow Art Theatre for bringing it into line, in their original production of it in January, 1904, with some of his earlier plays, as a 'sorrowful tragedy of Russian life', full of a vague melancholy. This first performance was made the occasion of a remarkable demonstration of affection for Chekhov on the part of theatre and public, a final triumph, six months before his death, but it does seem as if the producers, Stanislavsky and Nemirovich-Danchenko, did not sufficiently allow for his intention this time to stress the comedy in his tragi-comedy, or rather the juxtaposition of the tragic and the comic, which, as he protested, he found associated in real life.

Their mistake was after all natural enough, for there had been no essential change in Chekhov's technique. Here, as before, we have the 'ingeniously haphazard methods of revealing human nature', the avoidance of dovetailing dialogue and of everything conventionally 'stagey', the evocation of emotion through symbols directed both to eye and ear, mysterious ones sometimes, like the sound as of a breaking string, heard dying away on the air in Act II, which fills all who hear it with a vague foreboding, as in German fate-dramas a century before. In the masterly third act in particular the producers saw another example of Chekhovian atmosphere, intended to convey to the audience, by a combination of devices, the emotions of Mme Ranevsky, on tenterhooks for the result of the auction.

In the atmosphere of a not very cheerful evening party [the biographer of Nemirovich-Danchenko writes] to the accompaniment of waltz music and Charlotte's noisy 'conjuring', the agonising suspense of Mme Ranevsky grew and grew, only heightened by the confident assurances of Anya and Trofimov, who have no longer any use for the cherry orchard. The excitement rose to a climax, then it seemed it might be resolved at any moment, and again a new convulsive tightening was produced, through a mere trifle, through the sound of billiard balls heard from the neighbouring room, which prevented Gaev from telling his sister how the auction had ended. And rising to its highest tension, the mood of the act was relieved at last by the drunken 'I have bought it' of Lopakhin, the quiet weeping of Mme Ranevsky, the snatches of consoling words from Anya. So with the end of the act came the end of an epoch and the beginning of a new one, in which there will be no room for the former owners of the Cherry Orchard.

But this interpretation, stressing the social revolutionary element in the play in its effect on an individual, did not do full justice to the complexity of the 'vaudeville', the tragi-comedy of life which Chekhov evidently meant to suggest, and which we are perhaps better able to appreciate after the subtle use made of symbolism in many more recent dramas. As in Giraudoux, the apparently nonsensical conveys a sense of the unanalysable strangeness of life, together with a Russian warmth of human feeling for the 'soul' even in grotesques like Charlotte, a waif whose clowning masks her loneliness, or Simeonov-Pishchik and Gaev, victims of circumstances and of the temperament that nature gave them. Like so many figures we have noticed in the stories, from *A Daughter of Albion* onwards, they make us laugh, but a little reflection shows us a core of humanity in the most ridiculous of them, as in Shakespeare's clowns and madmen, and makes us less inclined to interpret the works in which they occur in terms of any ready-made philosophy.

If Chekhov's most devoted contemporary admirers sometimes failed so badly in interpreting his intentions, it is not surprising to find, as was noted in our Introduction, that in Russia to-day he is still read in many different ways, or that English and Russian critics have usually stressed quite different aspects of his art. One of his most sensitive readers in this country, Virginia Woolf, wrote of him, for instance: 'Our first impressions of Chekhov are not of simplicity but of bewilderment', and her feeling has been widely shared. A recent Russian biographer on the other hand, Derman, finds it difficult to imagine a Russian reader to whom Chekhov would be incomprehensible, so great is the simplicity of his thought and expression, a directness comparable with Pushkin's. His effect on succeeding writers has been almost as revolutionary as was Pushkin's, for here were the beginnings of a 'democratisation of art'. To understand how such radical divergences are possible in the views taken of one writer, we must remind ourselves that the reader is himself responsible for half of the effect produced by what he reads. The same symbols evoke varying meanings in the minds that bring them to life again, for though the readers must have something in common to give the words any meaning at all, they may differ almost without limit in their dispositions, memories and habits of thought. As to English bewilderment, there was always a great deal in Chekhov, his stories of children and animals, for instance, that no reader can ever have found bewildering at all, and much of the rest has lost its first strangeness for readers familiar with his imitators. But with Chekhov, as with any foreign writer, we cannot feel quite at home without learning something about his world, and to do him justice as an artist, we must distinguish between the early sketches he threw off with careless ease and the finished masterpieces of his maturity.

Despite all differences of interpretation, few would now dispute Chekhov's claim to a place among the major writers of the nineteenth century. 'Genius can be bounded in a nutshell and yet embrace the whole fullness of life', said Thomas Mann, shortly before his death, with reference to Chekhov, whom he had recently come to admire as much as his own first models, Balzac and Tolstoy. He now held Chekhov's best stories to be just as perfect within their limits as the monumental works of these great novelists, for perfection is independent of size. There is certainly something uniquely impressive in the epic breadth of a Tolstoy, something for which Chekhov strove, we have seen, in vain, and though his own narrow angle pictures, put side by side, cover no less wide a span than Tolstoy's novels, they are not organized in relation to each other to form worlds of the imagination such as those that confront us in *Anna Karenina* or *War and Peace*. But against that consideration, to be just, we must set his mastery in the drama, where he is incomparably greater than Tolstoy. The acquired habit of extreme brevity, the lack of a unified philosophy, the interruption of his work by illness, all these things help to explain his abandonment of the projected novels, but what mattered most was probably the perfection of his sense of form, combined with the personal modesty and absolute honesty which endeared him to his friends and which those who know him well through his works and letters still find irresistible. Tolstoy the artist is magnificent, but from the would-be prophet we are often repelled by what Mann calls his 'colossal conceit'. The 'gentle ironist' Chekhov, with no gospel to offer but tolerance and humanity, by the reticence and purity of his art has a no less enduring appeal.

APPENDIX

1860   Born at Taganrog.
1869–79   Pupil at the Taganrog Classical Gymnasium.
1876   Parents leave Taganrog for Moscow.
1879–84   Medical studies at Moscow University.
1881–87   Contributor to Moscow and St Petersburg humorous journals.
1884   Hospital work as young medical graduate. Collection *Tales of Melpomene.*
1885   First visit to St Petersburg.
1886   Contributor to *New Times.* Collection *Motley Tales.* Letter from Grigorovich.
1887   Collections *In the Twilight* and *Innocent Talk.* Journey to South Russia. *Ivanov* performed at Korsch Theatre, Moscow.
1888   Contributor to *Northern Courier. The Bear* and *The Proposal* performed. Awarded half of the Pushkin Prize. Collection *Tales.*
1889   *Ivanov* at Alexandrovsky Theatre, St Petersburg. *The Wood Demon* at Abramova Theatre, Moscow.
1890   (April to December) Journey to Sakhalin.
1891   Holiday in Vienna, Florence, Rome, Monte Carlo, Paris.
1892   Famine relief work. Buys the estate of Melikhovo. Work on cholera committee. Contributor to *Russian Thought.*
1893   *Sakhalin Island* published in *Russian Thought.*
1894   Holiday in Italy. Collection *Tales and Stories.*
1895   First visit to Tolstoy.
1896   Journey to the Caucasus and the Crimea. *The Seagull* at the Alexandrovsky Theatre.
1897   Seriously ill with tuberculosis (first symptoms from 1883). Holiday at Biarritz and Nice.
1898   Builds house at Yalta, Crimea. *The Seagull* at the Moscow Art Theatre.
1899   Sale of copyright to the publisher Marx, leading to *Collected Works* in 14 volumes (1900–1904). Visit of Gorki. *Uncle Vanya* at the Moscow Art Theatre. Melikhovo sold.
1900   Elected to Moscow Academy of Sciences. Holiday in Nice.
1901   *The Three Sisters* at Moscow Art Theatre. Marriage to Olga Knipper. Visit with Gorki to Tolstoy.
1904   *The Cherry Orchard* at Moscow Art Theatre. 2 July: death at Badenweiler.

DATES OF INDIVIDUAL STORIES

1883   *Fat and Thin. A Daughter of Albion. A Classical Student. A Tragic Actor.*
1884   *The Tutor. Surgery*.*

1885	*Sergeant Prishibeyev*. Horse and Tremulous Doe*. The Dance Pianist*. A Dead Body. Boots. A Malefactor. The Fish. Sorrow. The Huntsman. Misery. The Cook's Wedding.*
1886	*Hush! Excellent People. An Actor's End. The Jeune Premier. In the Court. The Witch. Agafya. The Requiem. A Trivial Incident. On the Road. An Upheaval. Easter Eve. Dreams. Art. A Nightmare. The Husband. Ladies. The Privy Councillor. Anyuta. Ivan Matveich. The Chorus Girl. A Misfortune. The Teacher. In the Dark. A Blunder. A Joke. The Happy Man. A Tripping Tongue. Grisha. Children. Vanka. A Trifle from Life. The Chemist's Wife.*
1887	*The Old House. A Father. The Examining Magistrate. Enemies. Verochka. Happiness. Uprooted. The Steppe. The Kiss. The Cattle Dealers.*
1888	*The Beauties. A Story without a Title. Sleepy. A Nervous Breakdown. The Party. The Bet. Lights.*
1889	*A Dreary Story. The Princess.*
1890	*The Horse-stealers.*
1891	*The Duel. Peasant Wives.*
1892	*Ward No. 6. The Wife. In Exile. Neighbours.*
1894	*A Woman's Kingdom. The Teacher of Literature.*
1895	*Three Years.*
1896	*An Artist's Story.*
1897	*Peasants.*
1898	*The Man in a Case. Gooseberries. About Love. A Doctor's Visit. The Darling.*
1899	*The New Villa. On Official Duty.*
1900	*In the Ravine.*
1903	*The Betrothed*

SELECT BIBLIOGRAPHY

WORKS, LETTERS, NOTEBOOKS, REMINISCENCES

The most complete edition of the works and letters in Russian is the one which began to appear in 1944 (Moscow), *Works*, 1–12, 1944–1949, *Letters*, 8 vols, 1948–1951.

A full selection from the stories and plays was translated into English by Constance Garnett, 15 volumes, London, 1916–1923, and later.

Selections from the letters in: *Letters of Anton Tchehov*, translated by Constance Garnett, London 1920.

The Life and Letters of Anton Tchekhov, translated and edited by S. S. Koteliansky and Philip Tomlinson, London, 1925.

Letters of A. P. Tchehov to Olga L. Knipper, Translated by Constance Garnett, London, 1926.

Notebooks and reminiscences in: *A. Chekhov, Literary and Theatrical Reminiscences* [of Sobolev, Korolenko, Kuprin, Bunin, Andreyev etc.], London, 1927. *The Note Books of Anton Chekhov*, and M. Gorky, *Reminiscences of Chekhov*, London, 1921. *The Personal Papers of A. Chekhov*, introduction by M. Josephson, New York, 1948.

For other translations of small groups of stories and plays, see the bibliographical index in David Magarshack's *Chekhov*, complete to 1952.

BIOGRAPHY AND CRITICISM (IN ENGLISH)

Shestov, L., *Anton Chekhov and Other Essays*, translated by S. Koteliansky and J. M. Murry, Dublin, 1917.

Gerhardi, W., *Anton Chekhov, a Critical Study*, London, 1923.

Woolf, Virginia, 'The Russian point of view', in: *The Common Reader*, London, 1925.

Mirsky, D. S., *Modern Russian Literature*, London, 1925.
                Contemporary Russian Literature, London, 1926.

Elton, O., *Chekhov*. The Taylorian Lecture, Oxford, 1929.

Chukovsky, K., *Chekhov the Man*, translated by Pauline Rose, London, 1945.

Bruford, W. H., *Chekhov and his Russia*. A sociological study. London, 1947.

Hingley, Ronald, *Chekhov*. A biographical and critical study. (with full bibliography, also of Russian critical works), London, 1950.

Avilov, Lydia, *Chekhov in My Life*, translated, with an introduction by David Magarshack, London, 1950.

Némirovsky, Irène, *A Life of Chekhov*, translated by E. de Mauny, London, 1950.

Magarshack, David, *Chekhov the Dramatist*, London, 1952.
                   Chekhov, a Life, London, 1952.